The Financial Rules for New College Graduates

The Financial Rules for New College Graduates

Invest before Paying Off Debt—and Other Tips Your Professors Didn't Teach You

Michael C. Taylor

 PRAEGER™

An Imprint of ABC-CLIO, LLC

Santa Barbara, California • Denver, Colorado

Library of Congress Cataloging in Publication Control Number: 2017056898

ISBN: 978-1-4408-6105-5 (print)
    978-1-4408-6106-2 (ebook)

22 21 20 19   4 5

This book is also available as an eBook.

Praeger
An Imprint of ABC-CLIO, LLC

ABC-CLIO, LLC
130 Cremona Drive, P.O. Box 1911
Santa Barbara, California 93116-1911
www.abc-clio.com

This book is printed on acid-free paper ∞

Manufactured in the United States of America

Contents

PART 1

What's Stopping You from Achieving Wealth?

CHAPTER ONE

You Should Be Wealthy

You Should Be Wealthy

But, like 99% of us, you don't feel wealthy.

You can become wealthy, but you do not even know where to begin.

Even for those of us living in the wealthiest era in human history, even for those of us born by accident into one of the richest countries in the world, even so, the vast majority of us do not feel wealthy.

We see wealthy people as some other group, perhaps the athlete interviewed on ESPN after the game, or the actress in the sparkly gown receiving her second Academy Award on the stage, or those tech start-up guys announcing a strategic partnership with Google at the press conference. But many of us doubt that *we* could be part of the group of wealthy people.

Believe me, you can be wealthy.

The ideas here will—provided you're young, disciplined, and embrace the ideas in this book fully—make you wealthy over your lifetime.

Another Book about Getting Wealthy?

Yes, this is another book about getting wealthy.

You're *skeptical*. Skeptical is good. In fact, it's one of the three key traits for building wealth.

But before you turn too skeptical on me, let me give you a sneak-peek into another of the three key traits of wealthy people that you'll need to embrace to become wealthy: *optimism*.

Because if you don't have optimism, if you think becoming wealthy is something not for you, if you think to yourself "some few people get wealthy, but 99% of us don't, and there's just nothing new to say," well then, you're already defeated. You should just put this book down, keep the purchase money in your thin wallet, and let some other damned fool try it.

Or, I recommend a better choice: conserve your optimism for a little while longer and just read to the end of the chapter.

So yes, this is another book about getting wealthy. *Modestly* speaking, this wisdom has been said elsewhere. Where I think I can improve on that wisdom is with simple explanations of concepts that previously might have seemed difficult, but aren't; and with three main principles of thinking like a wealthy person woven into 21 thematic chapters, in a way you can use them.

Why Does Personal Finance Seem So Complicated?

We could choose to blame our parents and teachers and professors, who in an ideal world should have been able to teach us what we need to know, starting around junior high, with follow-up ideas every year.

I personally find our parents and teachers innocent of this fiasco. Most parents and teachers know just as little as we know about the path to wealth.

If you had a wealthy parent—a parent who knew how to teach you this stuff—you might not need to read this book. Also, incidentally, your first millions would come to you tax free! But we'll get to that in the chapter on taxes, Chapter 10.

So no, please do not blame "the adults" in your life.

So Who *Can* We Blame?

I personally blame financial media.

The majority of what we see on television, hear on radio, and read online about finance amounts to nonsensical babble and sales pitches. These do not help us get wealthy. In fact—in total and on balance—they keep us poor.

For the moment, I will spare you my full-on financial-media rant. But I'll only delay my rant until Chapter 2. We need to understand and properly filter financial media better because it's one of the keys to building wealth.

What I Want You to Learn from This Book, More Than Anything Else

For a smart person like you, personal finance is not complicated.

I can teach you how to think like a wealthy person.

With the right knowledge and attitude, you can be wealthy in your lifetime.

Each chapter of this book provides unique insight into a major personal financial topic, which might otherwise take decades to understand. A few highlights include:

- The *three attitudes of wealthy people* that you must adopt if you would like to be wealthy (Chapter 1).
- Advice on how to understand financial media, and most importantly *why you need to ignore most of it* (Chapter 2).
- The *most powerful math formula in the known universe*, taught and explained in a way so that you can use it yourself (Chapter 4).
- The *evil algebraic inverse twin* of that math formula, which underpins all fundamental investing (Chapter 5).
- Why *investing for retirement before paying off student loans* makes sense (Chapters 8 and 9).
- An explanation that there are really *only two kinds of investments in the world*, and how to figure out which of those two will work best for you in the long run (Chapter 14).
- The entire trillion-dollar personal investment industry sliced, diced, sautéed, and reduced to *the only two sentences that you'll ever need* in order to invest your money correctly (Chapter 14).
- The *single question you must always ask* before purchasing any kind of insurance (Chapter 16).
- A totally *free estate-planning tool you can use to pass on tax-free wealth* to your heirs (however undeserving those heirs may be) (Chapter 19).
- The *single best definition of "wealthy"* you'll ever read (Chapter 21).

The mission of this book is to show how specific (and *simple!*) choices you make, especially in the years after college, can *guarantee* you long-term wealth.

At the end of this book, if you embrace the ideas, you will know everything you need to know to be wealthy. I don't mean everything you could know, and I don't mean everything you might want to know, but rather everything you *need* to know to be wealthy. You will know this better than the athlete on ESPN, the actress at the Academy Awards, or the executives at the Google press conference. I promise you.

Everything you *need* to know about personal finance, at the end of the day, is simple.

Notice I didn't say *easy*, because it's not all easy to do. Unlike that Mega Abdominal-Cruncher available on late-night television (for just $24.99!), this isn't an "easy-peasy 6 minutes a day" cure-all to become the abdominal-flexing Charles Atlas of personal finance by next week.

Don't let me mislead you. The doing part, the actual daily and monthly and yearly choices to apply the attitudes of wealthy people to the simple principles throughout the rest of the book? That's hard.

If it were *easy* we would all already be wealthy. If it were *easy*, 55% of Americans with credit cards would not be carrying a balance month to month, undermining *any chance they have* of accumulating wealth. If it were *easy*, just 1% of Americans would not control one-third of the wealth in the country. If it were *easy*, the great majority of people would be wealthy. But we are not.

So please, do not confuse *simple* with *easy*.

But you can follow these principles, and you should. And if you do it, you'll be richer at the end of your life for it.

Are the Wealthy Really Different from You and Me?

That partly depends on what you do.

Wealthy people do not day-trade stocks. Wealthy people pay off their credit card balances every month. Wealthy people do not buy lottery tickets. Wealthy people do not buy too much insurance. Wealthy people do not seek to flip houses. Wealthy people understand the tax consequences of their financial choices. Wealthy people do estate planning.

All of these actions tend to keep wealthy people wealthy.

Now, I'm assuming you're smart, so you probably have this skeptical voice inside you that notices a possible teensy, tiny, flaw in my logic. Maybe, you're thinking, wealthy people do these "right actions" precisely because they can afford to.

So, is my logic bass-ackwards?

Maybe, you're thinking, wealthy folks don't day-trade stocks or flip houses because *they don't need the money*. Maybe, you're thinking, wealthy people pay their credit cards in full because *they actually have the money to pay every month*.

Fine, I understand your thought process. In a small way, and in the short run, yes, it is easier to do the right thing when there's money in the bank.

But for the most part, that's the wrong logic. The behaviors and choices of people lead to them becoming wealthy, not the other way around.

And what leads to the correct choices? It really comes down to three key attitudes: *modesty*, *skepticism*, and *optimism*.

Your Toolkit

What tools do you, the reader, need? Prior knowledge is not required, and attitude is everything. The three most important attitudes, for every aspect of financial knowledge, as I've already mentioned, are *modesty, optimism*, and *skepticism*. We'll return to these three key attitudes in every chapter throughout the book.

You may be wondering—why can't I just tell you the best personal finance choices upfront, rather than spend time describing wealthy-people attitudes first, and then laying out the best choices later?

My answer begins with the fact that individual circumstances differ substantially, and the right choices for you depend on your circumstances, your personality, your earning power, and your phase of life.

The right attitudes, however, remain constant. If you spend time cultivating and recognizing the attitudes of wealthy people, I'm confident you will make the right choices, and you will become wealthy.

How Is This Book Organized?

The 21 chapters reflect a logical prioritization of personal finance knowledge. Earlier chapters provide more of a foundation for learning to think like, and become, a wealthy person, than later chapters. Later chapters tend to link to practical decision making on a financial choice you face. I trust you will find the concepts in each chapter useful and universal enough that you can return to them at different financial stages of your life, as needed.

Although I've ordered the chapters according to what I think is a logical life progression, you do not need to read this straight through from start to finish. A perfectly good alternative would be the "choose your own adventure" approach, starting where you need help most, and then seeing which concepts or decisions arise next.

If you are going to purchase a car this week, for example, I recommend you just turn to the car-buying chapter (Chapter 11) first. Then, as you get ready to purchase insurance in later months or years, review that chapter (Chapter 16) as needed. If you are reading this and you're 14 years old, then you probably don't need to think about either retirement savings (Chapter 9) or estate planning (Chapter 19), so just skip those chapters for now.

Also, if you're reading this and you're 14 years old: Stop day-trading convertible bonds to kick-start your hedge fund, and go outside and play in the traffic. Come back when you're at least 18. Agreed? OK, great, talk to you then.

While concepts in some chapters build on earlier chapters, and the three attitudes of wealthy people thread throughout each chapter, the basic finance principles for each topic stand on their own.

Who Am I?

I'm a dad. I'm a citizen. I'm a consumer of financial news. I used to work on Wall Street, selling bonds for Goldman Sachs. I used to run my own investment fund, purchasing distressed debt. After Wall Street imploded in 2008, and after I shut my investment fund in the years following that, I began to write about finance.

Am I the Messiah of Money? The Raj of Riches? The Guru of Greed? No.

I would like this book to give you the opposite feeling you get from reading the "Look at me! Look how rich I am! Do what I do, and build yourself a big pile of money!" genre of self-help books.

No.

I aspire to something much more modest than all that. Personal finance should be nonmystical and uncomplicated. I'm deeply skeptical of gurus. Please, let me spare you their magical thinking. I'm optimistic you will learn more from my approach than that typical sales pitch.

Most of us, unless we've worked in finance, spend our lives muddling through on money topics, picking up a tip from a magazine here, grazing on a few ideas from a finance website there. When we need to make a decision, we turn to someone in our life who seems more money-oriented than we are, and generally we do what they recommend.

What a catastrophe this muddling approach has turned out to be.

When the last financial crisis hit, our collective indifference and ignorance almost blew up *everything*. It was not pretty. And for most people, finance continues to be *pretty* unpretty.

If only the bankers understand finance, I've come to realize—as a result of the last crisis—we've got a serious problem.

Who Is This Book For?

This book is for my daughters, as they grow, so they do not need to work on Wall Street to "get finance," and to later "get money."

For my fellow citizens, as they seek to understand our world better.

For everyone inundated with financial media, much of it wrong or misleading.

For anyone who wants a guide to personal finance, and high finance, explained jargon-free, and without any sales pitch.

For anyone who needs a finance buddy to break down the confusing world of finance into easy-to-understand attitudes and choices.

I wrote this book for educated people who are not experts in finance.

In that sense I've written this book for an alternate-universe me—someone who did not end up going to Wall Street after college but who wanted to know more about money and personal finance and, quite possibly, how to get wealthy.

But really, of course, I wrote this for you, so you don't have to work on Wall Street to feel like you know what to do with your finances. I wrote this for you, so that you know that being wealthy is not only possible, but you have the ability to make it happen in your lifetime.

For most people, I don't particularly recommend working on Wall Street, or founding your own investment fund. The world does not especially need more financiers.

The world does need, however, more financially savvy people. The world does, in fact, need more people to become wealthy.

In the end, what is the goal of learning about finance? I believe it's not to get rich—or at least not to get rich quick—but rather to have a lifelong, healthy, confident relationship with money, savings, wealth creation, and financial citizenship. That healthy, confident relationship will, incidentally, help you *grow your money slowly,* but as a natural consequence of your understanding.

CHAPTER TWO

On the Financial Infotainment Industrial Complex

The Media That Surrounds Us

Picture yourself for a moment in one of those extremely crowded open-air markets full of venders, selling everything from vegetables to live chickens to knitted sweaters, and you're trying to make your way through twice a day, every day, to get to work. A brightly colored handmade blanket obstructs your left-side vision, while on your right a bearded man in a robe appears to conduct an unseen orchestra in the air, shouting at high volume about his cheap calculators for sale. This is what all of us navigate, every day, from the Internet, radio, television, and newspapers.

Financial media bombards us like this open-air market. They tug at our sleeves. Their strobe lights flicker at our eyes.

"Come this way." "Have a look." "My friend, my friend, come under this curtain and join me for a cup of tea."

This mélange of oily salespeople, pirates, preachers, and circus clowns all offer a self-serving pitch.

When you work in finance, as I did, you quickly recognize that everyone who appears on financial media has something to sell. Those folks on television, radio, and online are not reasonable, helpful, guides to building wealth. They are not your friends. These are people hawking their wares.

The bond fund billionaire who inevitably concludes his monthly newsletter with the reasons we should buy bonds? He's selling his product, which happens to be *bond mutual funds*.

The Wall Street analyst who argues passionately and intelligently that all of her models indicate the energy and retail sectors are fundamentally cheap on a historical PE basis, and it's time to jump into energy and retail stocks with both feet? Trust me, you can forget about understanding PE ratios, because you don't need to understand a word she is saying. All you need to know is that she's selling something.

The permanently pessimistic hedge fund manager with a doom-and-gloom story about how the entire financial system will likely collapse next year? He's selling his product too, which is a hedge fund designed to make money when the market goes down.

The handsome insurance executive on your screen seemingly concerned about the dwindling Social Security fund, furrowing his brow about the need for individual retirement planning through annuities? You got it. He's selling.

Selling, selling, selling.

The Financial Infotainment Industrial Complex

I call this open-air market the Financial Infotainment Industrial Complex. Like the Military Industrial Complex before it, the Financial Infotainment Industrial Complex menaces our society. By keeping us credulous, or pessimistic, or pumped full of false confidence, this complex blocks us from building wealth.

Notice for a moment that the "experts" I'm warning you against, who are really salespeople in disguise, all come from the respectable worlds of journalism, money management, insurance, and banking. They are not fundamentally bad people, any more than the bearded guy shouting in the open-air market is a bad person. They are at the top of the Financial Infotainment Industrial Complex pyramid, and their job is to sell to you, rather than help you understand your financial world.

There is an even worse set of hucksters below the respectable ones, the ones who sell online "free seminars on house flipping," books with the words "secrets" and "millionaire" in the title, or pitch you on late night "increase your cash flow" classes. They are distinctly worse, depending as they do on exploitative, fraudulent pitches. But in a sense they are so obviously bad that I'm less focused on warning you about them.

I really mean to warn you about the seemingly reputable ones, the ones pretending to offer "expertise" when really they are pitching their products.

How can a person like you, someone who has not worked in finance, distinguish the buskers from the truth-tellers?

Throughout this book I will help you recognize truth when you see it. When you adopt the attitudes of a wealthy person—*modesty, skepticism, and optimism*—you will find yourself able to skip right past the open-air market of carny barkers.

This book is a map to a quiet, safe, well-lit street you hadn't noticed before, that will get you there and back, faster. This book aims to turn down the volume on all that unnecessary noise.

Do I Really Have to Stop Participating in the Financial Infotainment Industrial Complex?

But wait, you say, the open-air market is fun. What if you enjoy watching MSNBC and Fox Business News, or that guy who makes the whistles and honking clown noises while he keeps up a steady patter about stocks he's supposedly "buying" this week? What if you enjoy the heart-pumping rush of hitting "Enter" on your computer or phone to send a buy order through your stock-trading platform?

That's fine, I get it. Fun is fun. When I'm on vacation in another country, I like wandering slowly through open-air markets as well. But as you read this book, keep in mind that that adrenalin rush has nothing to do with getting wealthy, and instead is a form of entertainment.

If you don't mind losing a little bit of your money sitting down for a cup of tea under the vender's tent, then go for it. It *is* fun. But just so you know: it's the opposite of getting wealthy.

What's Up with This Media Critique Anyway?

Why do I care so much about thrusting my financial media critique in the beginning of a book about getting wealthy?

I care because you can't hope to adopt the attitudes of a wealthy person unless you understand the wrong messages we get surrounded by all day, every day.

We need to develop a very strong defense mechanism against the wrong attitudes, being sold to us all day long. When you do build that defense mechanism against the media—when you become *modest*, *skeptical*, and *optimistic*—wealth will follow.

PART 2

Finance Math Concepts for Life

CHAPTER THREE

On Interest Rates

Interest rates strike nonfinance people as so abstract that we need a meta-phor (or two) for understanding them. The point of this chapter is to provide a couple of metaphors you can use to understand what interest rates are, and what interest rates do. And ideally, how interest rates can make you wealthy or keep you poor.

Parenthetical Book Structure Thoughts

Stepping back from that short-term goal for one moment, however, I want to give some further guidance as to how this entire book is structured and how you can choose to read it.

This chapter and Chapters 4 and 5 that follow are the only "technical" parts of the book. By technical I mean they involve a little bit of math. In that sense, they would be greatly enhanced by opening up a spreadsheet and then by using the text as a sort of workbook to help you with that spreadsheet. The math is accessible to junior high or early high school students and never gets beyond the application of algebra. It also uses exponents, otherwise described as "a number raised to the power of another number."

However, to the math-allergic among you, I understand this could be as appealing to you as green olives and anchovies are to me.

So, let me preface this section with the following: Chapters 6 through 21 do not require any math to understand. You can grasp the main concepts without tickling your math-brain, and you can absolutely get wealthy applying the concepts and leaving behind your calculator and spread-sheet. If you find math terrifying, you have my permission to skip ahead to Chapters 6 through 21. Just promise me you'll eventually come back to the beginning?

Chapters 6 through 21 are greatly enhanced by an understanding of interest rates from this chapter and the math of Chapters 4 and 5. My justification for claiming that this book will make you money is built largely on an understanding of interest rates, compound interest, and discounted cash flows, the subjects of Chapters 3, 4, and 5.

The reasons I've placed the math in this book upfront—knowing it will turn off some readers—are that I feel extremely passionately that:

1. These are key finance tools everyone should have.
2. They are absolutely in reach of a reader like you.
3. Using these math tools will make a lifetime of good financial choices so much more likely. You won't need to depend on financial gurus to justify choices for you. You can work out the justification for yourself using the astonishing precision of mathematical truth.

OK, that's it for the moment on parenthetical book-structure notes. Let's get back to . . .

Interest Rates in Practice

Let's start with the basic mechanics of interest rates, before moving on to the theoretical and metaphorical.

If I lend my $100 to my neighbor Bob for a year at a 6% annual interest rate, the stated interest rate means that I will receive $6 back from Bob at the end of the year, in addition to my original $100, because $6 is 6% of the original $100.

Conversely, if I borrow $100 from Nina and agree to pay an 8% annual interest rate on the loan, I will owe Nina both the $100 back as well as $8, for a total of $108 at the end of 1 year.

Borrowing and lending money generally involves charging a percentage of the original amount as interest, which compensates the lender by returning a larger amount of money to him or her in the future.

Why does the lender need more money in the future than he or she had lent today?

Ah, so glad you asked.

The real answer is not—as you might first suspect—because lenders are greedy and covet more money. I mean, lenders might indeed be greedy, but that's not the reason for the practice of charging interest.

The real answer comes from the concept known as the time value of money.

The Time Value of Money Concept

OK, one more brief definitional segment before we get to the interest rate metaphors: the time value of money (TVM) concept says that money in today's terms *is always worth more* than the same amount of money in tomorrow's terms.

One way to understand this intuitively is to imagine you could be given the choice of receiving $1,000 today, or $1,000 sometime in the future, say, 5 years from now. Most people, the TVM concept posits, will want to receive $1,000 today, because it's inherently more valuable today than in the future. The "more value" comes partly from the fact that we could do stuff with the money today, and we can't really do stuff right now with money that's only going to arrive in 5 years.

The "more value" also partly comes from the fact that it's a risky world and we might never get a chance to receive the $1,000, either because we pass away or the person offering it may not be able to deliver on his or her promise.

A third reason for the TVM is that in many situations we lose the value of money through inflation—meaning we will be able to buy less with $1,000 in 5 years than we can buy today.

The commonsense cliché "a bird in the hand is worth two in the bush" approximately captures pretty well the TVM concept, highlighting that money we can have today is more valuable than some future money that we may or may not ever get to receive.

There are probably other reasons for the TVM, this idea that money today is more valuable than money in the future, but you don't necessarily need an economist's view for the TVM to work for you.

The main reason to know this for getting wealthy is that we need a way to link—mathematically—the value of money today with money in the future.

That is really what interest rates help us do.

OK, back to my interest rate metaphors.

The Bridge: Metaphor Number One

Functionally speaking, interest rates are a bridge.

The interest rate is the mathematical bridge that links money today to money in the future.

If we have money today, we can figure out precisely how much money we can turn that into at some future date, according to our interest rate. When our $100 today becomes $106 one year into the future, we need the 6% interest rate bridge to get there.

One main reason I want to use metaphors for talking about interest rates is that the concept of "interest rate" actually goes by many names, depending on the context. Yield, discount rate, return, and internal rate of return (IRR) are all related concepts that act as bridges between money today and money in the future.

All of these—interest rate, yield, discount rate, and IRR—do the same thing. All of these concepts refer to the number, usually expressed in annual percentage terms, that connects today's money to future money.

If we want to figure out how our $100 becomes a larger amount of money 14 months or 8 years or 38 years in the future, we will need to move from interest rate to these other concepts—yield, discount rate, and IRR—that all serve the same function. Mathematically, they all mean the same thing. They are the bridge between money today and money in the future.

The main points of Chapters 4 and 5—just to preview a bit more—are to explain how this mathematical bridge works in practice.

In Chapter 5 in particular, we can see how a known amount of money 38 years from now, for example, can link back, through our metaphorical interest rate bridge, to a precise amount of money today.

If I want to have $1,000,000 38 years from now, I think it's useful to know how to link that back to a specific amount of dollars today. With a 6% interest rate, or more precisely the equivalent concept of a 6% yield or 6% discount rate, I can immediately figure out, using a simple spreadsheet formula, that today's dollars have to be, specifically, $109,238.85.

Another way of stating that is to say I could start with just $109,238 today, earn a 6% annual compound return, and I will finish in 38 years from now, with $1,000,000. My reason for this chapter and Chapters 4 and 5 is that a 27-year-old, who has not yet planned on retirement at age 65 (but ought to!), might find this useful information to know.

The interest rate bridge—using the formulas we explore in Chapters 4 and 5—explains precisely how to calculate the change from money today into money in the future, as well as the reverse, how money in the future is equivalent to money today.

In mathematical terms, the bridge metaphor helps us connect two places: the present and the future, as it relates to money. With the bridge metaphor, we conceive of money turning into something else, money changing into something larger, as it crosses the bridge. Money travels from this side of the bridge to the other side. Money moves.

With the next metaphor, however, we conceive of ourselves as moving.

The Monorail: Metaphor Number Two

We are all, wittingly or not, *willingly or not*, dealing with money as we move through our lives. For many—OK, for the vast majority of us—money may seem like an impediment, a force that slows down our progress. If it wasn't for the need to reckon with money, we might think in our more frustrated moments, then we could really *get ahead* in life.

That frustrating feeling of pushing against a difficult force is the backward monorail many of us are on, as we pay interest on our debts.

You see, interest on money acts like a *moving monorail*, constantly either propelling you forward or pushing you back.

When you pay interest on your loans, for example, you're on that monorail. To pay back the $100 you borrowed, you'll need to come up with $106 at the end of the year, to use our earlier simple example of a 6% annual interest rate loan on $100. That extra money you have to produce is the force against you. It's the backward monorail that seems to keep you from getting ahead.

As we'll discuss in later chapters, the monorail is typically much tougher than that $6 on a $100 loan, for two reasons.

First, as we'll discuss in Chapter 6, borrowing rates are rarely as low as 6%, meaning the majority of us struggle to keep up against a much faster monorail than my simple example above. The average 12% rate on a credit card, or the typical maximum legally allowable 29.99% annual rate on credit cards, makes for very fast-moving monorails indeed.

The awful truth is that nobody who makes a practice of paying on high-interest credit cards will ever be able to *get ahead* against that difficult, backward-moving, monorail.

Second, as we'll talk about in Chapter 10, income taxes mean that many of us have to earn 25%–35% more than $106 just to pay back a $100 loan. What I mean is, if you pay a 30% income tax rate and you want to pay off your $100 debt, you'll have to work to earn $151.43.[1] The federal government will then collect its $43.45 (because that's 30% of earnings), leaving you with $106, sufficient to repay your loan.

So in effect, paying back the $100 loan will cost you not $106 but rather $151.43.

Between taxes and high interest, you end up having to sprint against a moving monorail just to try to stay in one place.

That's some depressing news.

Getting Ahead on the Monorail

But here's an optimistic thought: the monorail also moves the other way. Interest rates on your money—also broadly understood as yield and return—can move you forward. When interest rates work in your favor—specifically, when *you* are a lender or an investor—your money today grows into larger amounts in the future without you hardly even trying.

---

[1]If you're looking for the quick math I did to come up with $151.43 pretax earnings (PTE), the formula I used is just the amount of net after-tax money (NATM) divided by 1 minus the tax rate (TR) Algebraically you could write this as PTE = NATM/(1–TR). So, $106/(1–30%) gets me to $151.43.

If you have accumulated savings available for investment—and we'll talk in Chapter 13 about the specific conditions for that—then you can hop on the forward-moving money monorail. Without much effort you will get ahead—you will be propelled ahead by the growth of your own money.

For wealthy people, money they have today for investment simply grows into larger amounts of money tomorrow. For wealthy people, they can choose a slow-moving and safe monorail, historically earning 1% to 3% annual return, or they can choose a more volatile but ultimately faster monorail, earning above 5% per year. Done correctly, this wealth building requires little skill or effort.

I use the monorail metaphor to present this phenomenon because wealthy people with the right approach to investing cannot prevent themselves from having more money in the future. Just by standing still. Just by doing absolutely nothing. Money just grows on money, pretty much all by itself, if we can get ourselves out of the way and let it. If that sounds like something you might be interested in, read on.[2]

Preparing for Math: A Preview

The math formula of the next two chapters depends on four things, each of which I've introduced in metaphorical terms in this chapter. Math, the language of symbolic variables, is just a further abstraction of my metaphors.

Using the bridge metaphor, the four variables are:

1. Money today (on the close side of the bridge)
2. Money in the future (on the far side of the bridge)
3. Interest rate (the bridge itself)
4. Time (moving from one side of the bridge to the other)

In the next chapter I introduce shorthand letters for these variables, in order:

1. PV—present value—aka "money today"
2. FV—future value—aka "money in the future"
3. Y—yield—aka "interest rate," "discount rate," "IRR," or "the bridge itself"
4. N—time, in the form of the number of compounding periods

---

[2]My favorite faux-philosopher Jack Handey has a great line that sums up how the monorail does, and does not, work for you, depending on whether you are wealthy already or not. "It's easy to sit there and say you'd like to have more money. And I guess that's what I like about it. It's easy. Just sitting there, rocking back and forth, wanting that money."

Just to complete the preview, and to acclimate you to the most powerful mathematical force in the known universe, I want to write out the math formula that shows how money grows inevitably, powerfully into the future. I feel very strongly that spending a little bit of time with this formula—ideally engaging with it in a spreadsheet—can help incentivize you to get off the backward-moving monorail of debt and get you on the forward-moving monorail of wealth.

The compound interest formula we'll explore in Chapter 4:

$$FV = PV * (1 + Y)^N$$

That's it?

Yup, that's it.

We'll address this in (excruciating) detail in the next chapter.

In the meantime, I hope to inspire you to examine whether the monorail you are currently on—the interest rates that affect you and your money—moves you forward or whether it moves you backward. I hope you embrace the optimistic thought that even if right now you find yourself working twice as hard just to stay in one place on a backward-moving monorail, you can flip that switch. In the future, you could let yourself be propelled forward by the same monorail.

It's not easy to do, but it's also not complicated to understand.

CHAPTER FOUR

On Compound Interest

In the last chapter I leaned heavily on metaphors to introduce the meaning of interest rates, as either a bridge or a moving monorail. So let's do it again, but this time let's use metaphors for compound interest.

What Is the Point of Learning about Compound Interest?

Most simply, money grows on money.

We can understand this through metaphors of snowballs, or kittens, or pine trees.

Let's Start with Snowballs

The process begins slowly like a tiny ball of sticky snowflakes at the top of a mountain. But the gathering momentum of the little snowball causes new snow to stick to it. The larger ball of ice and snow packs itself tighter and adds new fresh powder to the outside, until both gravity and the natural mutual attractiveness of wet snow builds on its own momentum.

Like a downhill rolling snowball, after a while you cannot stop money from growing on its own. Wealth causes wealth, just as a mass of snow grows inevitably bigger as it falls down the mountain, aggregating through gravity.

You don't have to work to create the snowball of wealth; you just have to get out of the way.

To start, though, you do have to get to the top of the mountain to kick over a few sticky snowflakes. We'll talk more about that "getting started" part in Chapter 7.

What about Kittens?

In my backyard a few years ago, I noticed a stray feral cat, and I decided to ignore it. Well, *it* turned out to be a *her*. True story. One night I awoke at some gawdawful witching hour to a screeching that made me want to rip my ears out. Just over two months later, I noticed that same stray had become a mamma cat, jealously guarding a spot under my porch that contained her three babies. Stupid me, not understanding the compound interest principal of kittens, I ignored mamma cat and her babies, after she moved them away from under my porch. Out of sight, out of mind, I thought.

Well, less than a year later, six feral adult cats and three more kittens made my backyard their home. At that point I awoke to the mathematical nightmare of compound interest and called in a neighbor's help. We managed to get them all fixed and broke the mathematical cycle, but I hope you can see how that was on the verge of getting out of control.

Or a Pine Forest?

Both runaway snowballs and multiplying feral kittens sound a bit frightening to me. Let me introduce a happier metaphor to the growth of money due to compound interest. Picture a lone pine tree on an open plain. That lone tree will drop hundreds (maybe thousands?) of pinecones over the course of a season, and some of those cones may find the right mix of soil and water to sprout a new pine tree. From then on, the nascent pine forest cluster does not necessarily grow one at a time, but rather through a multiplier effect. As trees reach maturity and drop new pinecones, the growth of that forest accelerates. Assuming positive climate conditions, the pine forest grows inevitably and inexorably. After a little while, the forest growth does not depend on that first original pine tree, but rather grows based on the pine trees that came later. Over time this effect, slowly in the early years, but inevitably faster and powerfully in later years, is how compound interest grows our money.

Mathematically Speaking, What Is Compound Interest?

Mathematically, we want to calculate how the money that we have *right now in the present* becomes a larger amount of money *some time in the future*, through the intervention of time and a specific interest rate.

Let's Start with Regular Interest

If we have $1,000 right now in the present, and we grow that money for one year at 6%—through a 6% loan for one year to a friend, for example—then we expect to have $1,060 in the future.

I calculated that one-year future amount by multiplying the 6% annual interest rate by $1,000 to get $60, or

$$\$1,000 \times 0.06/\text{year} = \$60/\text{year}.$$

In the case of a loan to a friend—assuming all goes well—we get our $1,000 back, and we get the $60 interest, for the total of $1,060.

Now, Compound Interest

But that example above is not compound interest; that's just regular interest.

Compound interest kicks in during a second year, in which we might loan out our $1,060 to a different friend, who also agrees to pay us 6% in interest for the year.

After the second year, we expect to receive back $1,123.60.

Why?

Because we will earn $63.60 in interest in the second year, which I calculated as $1,060 \times 0.06 = \$63.60$. That interest, plus the original $1,060, makes $1,123.60.

So What?

So what I really want to point out is that the tiny kitten, mini snowball, or pine tree sapling is that extra $3.60 interest that we earned based on our additional $60 in principal in Year 2. That $3.60 can be called *interest on interest*.

The metaphor and mathematics of compound interest are always the story of earning *interest on interest*.

Jack Handey, my favorite faux-philosopher, quipped: "I believe in making the world safe for our children, but not our children's children, because I don't think children should be having sex."

See, that's exactly the way I feel about feral kittens in my backyard and under my porch. You could say Jack and I are morally opposed to those cats having sex.

When it comes to money, however, each new generation of money is quite fecund, meaning it multiplies itself, through compound interest year after year, and that's something I do approve of morally and financially. It's also something I think everyone should figure out how to calculate mathematically.

OK, Now Back to the Math

If we continued to track the growth of our money for another year at 6% we could watch our $1,123.60 become $1,191.02 after Year 3.

I calculate that by multiplying 6% by $1,123.60 to make $67.42 in interest, and then adding that to our starting value of $1,123.60 from Year 2.

With each compounding year, our original snowball of $1,000 begins to gain momentum, and grows at a faster rate than the year before. The 6% growth rate stays the same, but the results accelerate because each year's 6% growth is on a larger starting point.

If you chart the growth of compounding money, you see one of those curves that creeps upward slowly at first and then bends more steeply upwards until it reaches nearly a vertical trajectory.

Population growth curves work this way. Feral kittens in the backyard—left to their own devices—work this way. And thankfully, money works this way.

The hard part here is not to have your money grow on money. No, money is like kittens, snowballs, and pine trees. That happens naturally. The hard part is just getting started, and then getting out of the way.

My Deepest Mathematical Wish

Now we've gotten to what I really, really, wish to teach you about the compound growth of money:

You can calculate exactly how much your money will grow over time, all by yourself.

Traditionally, we think this must be some mystical process, demonstrating an advanced illusionist trick combined with technical wizardry well beyond our mortal ken. Do you have to be a seventh level magic user with 95 hit points and a *Princess Morgatha's Cloak of Invisibility* to do this? No! You do not.

We've been trained by the Financial Infotainment Industrial Complex to think investment advisers perform some magic trick when they present us how "If you invest X dollars for Y amount of time and earn Z amount of annual return, you can expect W amount of wealth by the time you retire."

What I want you to remember is that the main illusionist trick is to make this simple math seem complicated.

By the way, how do you benefit if you can do this math yourself? I'll tell you why.

If you can do this math, maybe, just maybe, you'll be unimpressed enough with your investment adviser's magic trick to demand lower fees. The investment adviser didn't really make you the money. Your money just multiplied like feral kittens, while your investment adviser took the credit for making it grow. That would be like me pretending to run a feline dating service in my backyard and charging heavy fees for it. I'd just be faking it and overcharging those kittens. Does that make sense?

The Math Formula for Compound Interest

In its simplest application, the following section can show you the magic trick.

For best results, I recommend opening a spreadsheet—like right now—for calculating the following algebraic formula.

For a simple demonstration, let's assume we have three variables, and one unknown variable.

The unknown variable we want to solve for is "how big will our money become at some point in the future?"

Let's call this variable future value, or **FV** for short.

The three known variables are:

- How much do we have now? Let's call this present value, or **PV** for short.
- At what annual percentage return does our money grow? Let's call this annual yield, or **Y** for short.
- How many years does our money grow? Let's call this number of compounding periods, or **N** for short.

I'll skip all the math proofs, but if we know the last three variables, we can calculate the original unknown variable future value, FV, through the following formula.

$$FV = PV * (1 + Y)^{\wedge}N$$

Look at that! That's it!

Isn't it amazing? The sky opens up and angels sing! Harmonic galaxies crash together while symphonic worlds collide in mathematical understanding! This is the powerful financial lever that Archimedes needed when he wanted to move planets!

No? Not really?

OK, let's do some examples and maybe that will help.

But seriously—like I mentioned above—you should work through these examples with a spreadsheet.

Trust me when I tell you that you cannot possibly understand this by simply reading the words and numbers. But also trust me that you could understand this if you open up a spreadsheet next to this book, and then use these words like a cookbook to take you step-by-step through the calculations. If you do that, you'll see there's not much complicated about it at all.

Working with a spreadsheet, you'll be able to watch the poetic mysteries of compounding pine forests, snowballs, and feral kittens unfold before your very eyes.

OK, I've already mentioned the importance of opening up a spreadsheet four times. This is my fifth and last time but I'm just saying, please, do the thing.

Kittens Again!

Let's say I have 4 feral kittens terrorizing my back yard. And let's say that on an annual basis, the population of kittens in my backyard grows by 50%. After 10 years, how many kittens will I have?

With that information we can use the compound interest formula to give us a precise answer.

The number of kittens we have today, 4, is the present value (PV).

The growth rate of kittens, 50%, is the rate of return, or yield (Y).

The number of compounding periods in years, 10, is our (N).

We plug those three variables into the formula

$$FV = PV * (1 + Y)\char94 N$$

to find out the future number of kittens (FV).

Future number of kittens = $4 * (1 + 0.5)\char94 10$

In my spreadsheet I calculate the answer of the future number of kittens (FV) = 230 kittens (plus some fractional amount of kittens, which I interpret as kittens still in utero). Talk about a loud feline ROAWR!

I am so glad I got those backyard kittens fixed.

(Psst. If you haven't opened up the spreadsheet yet, now would be a really great time to do so. Damnit, I broke my pledge of silence already.)

In one of the boxes in your spreadsheet you can type "=4*(1.5)^10" and see if you don't also get 230 (and change).

If you are mildly comfortable with spreadsheet programming, you could generalize the kittens example by creating boxes for inputting a different number of original kittens (PV), their growth rate (Y), and how many years they reproduce (N).

Once you've accomplished that, you'll be well on your way to mastering the most powerful financial math in the universe.

Snowballs

One caveat to this example: I understand the physics of this example probably makes no sense in the real world. I'm just using it to illustrate that compound growth can occur, and can be calculated, in terms other than money. Or feral kittens. Also, that you can start with small numbers, "compound grow" them at a particular rate many times, and the numbers get really, really big.

Our snowball begins rolling down a deep snowy slope high up in the Himalayas with a mass of one-quarter of a pound. Just 4 ounces. The size of a tiny 99-cent hamburger from McDonald's. This rolling quarter-pounder snowball gains weight at a rate of 10% for every 10 yards it rolls. How heavy is my snowball after it travels 1 mile down the mountain?

(At which point, it rolls off a high cliff, and drops dramatically into a high mountain lake below the cliff. Splash!)

We have enough information to figure out the final size of the snowball when it flies off the cliff. The starting value (PV) is 0.25 pounds. The rate of return, or yield (Y), is 10%.

The number of compounding periods (N) requires an additional step to calculate because I used 10-yard increments. Since I know there are 1,760 yards in a mile, and growth occurs every 10 yards, I can figure that we will have 176 compounding periods (N).

Again, just like kittens, we figure out the future snowball size (FV) using $FV = PV * (1 + Y)^N$.

$$FV = 0.25 * (1 + 0.1)^{176}$$

Using my spreadsheet again, I calculate my snowball grows to a little bit over 4.8 million pounds. What? That's a little bigger than the size of the Space Shuttle. Is my spreadsheet broken?

No. It's just that you can start with really small numbers, and if you compound at a fast enough rate and enough times, you end up with outrageously large numbers. In a weird way, this is important to remember when considering how to get wealthy. You can start super small, and with enough time and a large compound growth rate you end up really, really, big.

Kittens and snowballs are maybe a little scary though. Let's try something peaceful, calm, sleep inducing. Breathe deeply and imagine the aromatherapy that accompanies our next example.

Pine Tree Becomes a Forest

We start with a lone pine tree. Our forest grows at an annual rate of 5% per year. We check back in with our tree 50 years later and we find 11 trees total in our tiny forest, because $FV = 1 * (1 + 0.05)^{50}$, which my spreadsheet calculates for me is 11 trees (and change).

If we checked back with our slow-growth forest 200 years after our initial lone pine, we would find 17,292 trees (and change) because the future value $(FV) = 1 * (1 + 0.05)^{200}$.

If we checked back with our little forest after 500 years have passed—assuming growth stays steady at 5%—we'd find over 39 billion trees. That's calculated in my spreadsheet as $1 * (1 + 0.05)^{500}$.

I find this kind of interesting, and I hope you do too. It takes a while—the first 50 years—to get some traction for the forest, which only has 11 trees after half a century. But the way compound growth works is that 10 times 50 years doesn't resemble 10 times the growth. Compound growth—even modest 5% annual growth—leads to a whole other ridiculously large outcome in the long run.

Now, given enough time, the same principle would apply to $1. Your dollar, continuously invested for 500 years with a 5% growth rate, would become $39 billion. Again, it kind of doesn't matter how small you start. The compound interest formula shows the magic effect of time.

Now I think we're ready to move from kittens, snowballs, and forests back to our original project, of getting sophisticated about money, and maybe (just maybe!) getting wealthy over time.

Your skeptical mind might object to a few assumptions in my examples above, like the idea that the snowball grows at 10%, and you're thinking: does money grow at 10%? You're right to be skeptical. Or like the pine forest growing for 500 years, and you're thinking: I'm not a vampire, so I don't have 500 years to grow my money. You're also right. But these melodramatic examples and assumptions illustrate the extremes that compound growth can get to.

Practical Examples of the Application of Compound Interest Calculations to Money

We also need down-to-earth examples of compound interest interacting with real-world money situations. I want to offer you a sense for how we can apply the most powerful math in the universe to practical money situations.

The Growth of Government Debt

If the federal government has $1 trillion in debt today, and owes an average of 4% annual interest on its obligations, how much will this grow to in 5 years? To keep the math simple, assume the government is allowed to skip making interest payments for 5 years, but that the debt will compound each year.

From this scenario, we know the three variables of money today (PV), interest rate or yield (Y), and number of years compounding (N). And we can use those to plug into the compound interest formula to discover the future amount of debt, (FV), via the equation $FV = PV * (1+Y)^N$.

The future amount of government debt will be

$$= \$1 \text{ trillion} * (1+0.04)^5$$

As always with the compound interest formula, this is best done with a spreadsheet open. Plugged into a spreadsheet, I find the result of $1.216653 trillion. Or in other words, if you are a political leader looking to score points in the media by using math to your advantage—OUR GOVERNMENT WILL INCUR OVER $216 BILLION IN MORE DEBT OVER THE NEXT 5 YEARS! AHGG EVERYBODY SHOULD PANIC!

OK, deep breathing, not really. It's just math.

Future projections using the compound interest formula about the growth of money can come up with some big numbers in the future. Incidentally, people who don't understand compound interest math are more likely to be manipulated by leaders who cynically use big scary numbers for their purposes. But hopefully by now, not you and me.

So compound interest can often seem scary when talking about debts. On the other hand, it can seem exciting when talking about wealth.

Speaking of wealth, let's look at examples from a happier angle. What if your small amounts of money in a retirement account were allowed to grow over a long period of time?

The Growth of My IRA Contribution

Let's say I'm a 25-year-old, struggling this year to barely accumulate a little annual surplus that I can sock away in an IRA account.

(More on "how to actually save this amount of money" in Chapter 7, "Why an IRA" in Chapter 9, and "How to Invest" in Chapters 13 and 14.)

This can be relatively hard to do at age 25. But is it worth it?

What's that $5,000 going to become in the future? And how could that possibly make a difference in my life, in the long run?

I'm so glad you asked those questions.

Because the compound interest formula tells us exactly what my little $5,000 could become in the future.

We know the PV is $5,000. We can make an annual return (Y) assumption of anything we like, but let's say 8% just for fun. And let's look at the growth of this account by the time I turn 75, or in other words, 50 years of compounding (N).

To solve the formula and find out how much that little IRA contribution grows to in the future (PV) we plug in numbers into the $FV = PV * (1 + Y)\string^N$ formula in a spreadsheet.

The (FV) future value of my contribution becomes $5,000 * (1 + 0.08)\string^50$.

Which my spreadsheet tells me is $234,508.

I don't know about you, but to me that seems like a lot of money, for just one year's measly $5k contribution. If I could make a few years of contributions like that, you can easily see that millionaire status becomes a certainty for me in my old age. That's a neat trick. And it doesn't require hiring any fancy investment guru doing amazing stock picking at high costs. It just requires understanding a little bit of compound interest math.

Inflation over Time

Just as our money grows over time, inflation works in a compounding way to erode the value of our currency. We can use the compound interest formula to understand the change in prices due to inflation.

Let's say we need to know the future price of monthly rent in an apartment in our city, which currently rents for $1,000 per month. Every year the landlord raises the rent by 10%. What will the apartment cost us in the future, say, 15 years from now?

The inflation in our monthly rent can be calculated because we know the present rent (PV) of $1,000, we know the annual growth (Y) of 10%, and we know the number of compounding periods (N) from now that we need to calculate is 15. The future rent (FV) is calculated as PV $* (1+Y)$^N.

So, the future rent is $1,000 $* (1+0.10)$^15.

My spreadsheet solves this to tell me my rent in 15 years will be $4,177.25. Good to know.

I'm glad my IRA will be large enough to pay off that rent. Or, at least I will commit to it being large after I finish reading Chapter 7.

Calculating the growth of retirement savings, or government debt, or the effect of inflation are some of the practical applications of compound interest math. They are, admittedly, more useful to your financial life than calculating kittens, snowballs, and pine forest growth.

But I Want More!

There's more to say about compound interest math, and I'm eager to tell you about its evil inverse twin, discounted cashflows, in the next chapter.

If you want to dig deeper into compound interest, I recommend the Appendix for this chapter to add a layer of math complexity to the topic.

If you are a visual learner and want to join me through a video explanation, I'd also recommend you go to my website:

http://www.bankers-anonymous.com/blog/compound-interest-a-deeper-dive

for a deeper dive.

Concluding Thoughts

The compound interest formula explained in this chapter forms one-half of what I like to call "The Most Powerful Financial Math in the Known Universe." It explains everything from the growth of inflation such as in rental costs, to government debt, to the cost of credit card payments over time. More optimistically, it can explain how modest contributions to a retirement account at an early age can guarantee that we will become millionaires many times over by the time we retire. It's not magic or wizardry, it's just pretty simple math.

As I said you don't *have* to do this math yourself to benefit from the lessons of this book. But optimistically speaking, if you did master this, I think you would find yourself incentivized to do the right things with savings and investments.

The next chapter takes the same algebra formula and simply reverses it. The reversal allows us to figure out how money in the future can be valued as money today.

Appendix

In this Appendix, I assume you have already read or understand Chapter 4 on compound interest on kittens, snowballs, pine forests, retirement savings, inflation, and government debt.

This Appendix offers a practical illustration of how investors might use compound interest math when it comes to bond and stock calculation.

I also return to feral cats, and then the extraordinary potential profitability of credit card debt, for banks.

More Frequent Compounding than Annual Compounding

Now, are you ready to become a next-level, compound-interest-calculating Jedi?

Because in the real world of financial calculations, we need to introduce one more easy little step to achieve better precision with our numbers.

In many situations, money does not compound annually, but rather more than once a year. When you look at the real world, you realize compounding occurs more frequently than annually, like:

•   Bonds—usually 2 times a year

•   Dividend stocks—usually 4 times a year

•   Feral kittens (with their 60-day gestation period)—6 times a year, or

•   Credit card debt—12 times per year

To calculate more-often-than-annual compounding, we have to make sure the yield or annual growth number (Y) gets properly divided by the number of periods per year (which I'll call "p"). The compound interest formula I've been using could now be written with that extra tweak as $FV = PV * (1 + Y/p)^N$.

The innovation here with more-than-annual compounding is that p modifies the annual yield, and N becomes not the number of years but rather the total number of compounding periods.

This isn't complicated, and some examples will show exactly how this is done.

But again, don't just read the words on the page here—I still recommend opening up a spreadsheet and doing it alongside me.

Growth of Your Investment with a Dividend-Paying Stock

Let's say I own a stock that pays dividends 4 times per year. The stock costs me $50 and I buy just one share.

Now, here's a little fine print so that I can keep the math legit. Let's assume the following conditions:

1. The stock is part of a dividend reinvestment plan, also known as a DRIP. (More on this in Chapter 13, but suffice it to say that DRIPs are awesome. If you must buy individual stocks, enroll in an automatic dividend reinvestment plan).

2. The stock has a 4% annual dividend yield, which just means that right now it pays $2 per year in dividends (because 4% of $50 is $2. Stick with me here, this isn't getting any more complicated than this).

3. Quarterly dividends—a dividend payment every three months—would be $0.50, because that's one-quarter of $2 (but you knew that).

4. I can buy fractional amounts of shares (meaning less than a share if I have less than $50), which is generally allowed with DRIPs programs.

5. The stock doesn't go up in price at all over the next 40 years—it just stays the same price.

OK, I'm finally getting to my question now. If the stock doesn't go up in price, but I just reinvest my dividends in the same stock, how much is my investment worth 40 years from now?

The simple annual compound interest formula we used earlier in the chapter would suggest that my original amount of $50 (PV = $50) grows at 4% per year (Y = 4%) for 40 years (N = 40), so we would plug those numbers into the formula $FV = PV * (1 + Y)^N$.

Using the simple formula from before, my spreadsheet would tell me the answer is $50 * (1 + 0.04)^{40}$, which is $240.05

Now, there are two important things to say about my investment growing to $240.05. The first thing is that I've grown the initial $50 by 4.8 times my original investment over 40 years, without the stock appreciating in value at all. Almost quintupling my money, on just reinvested dividends. I think that fact alone is pretty interesting.

The second thing to say is that I haven't actually done the calculation correctly, which gets me back to the original point of this section on more-frequent-than-annual compounding.

Because I got paid quarterly dividends, my investment actually grows a little bit faster than it would with annual compounding, since it compounds slightly more often. The money I receive after just three months gets reinvested in more shares, so it has more time to grow than if I received my dividend just once a year.

To do the right calculation, note that my annual yield (Y) should be divided by a number that I called in the formula above p (p = 4) to reflect the fact that I get quarterly payments.

My 4-times-a-year Y therefore is 1.0%, which is just 4% divided by 4 (but you knew that already).

Over 40 years, my stock investment actually compounds at 1.0% a total of 160 times, because 4 times per year for 40 years is 160 compounding periods. My N therefore is 160.

The correct future value of my dividend-paying stock investment would actually be $50 * (1 + 0.01)^160.

That, my spreadsheet tells me, is $245.69. Which is slightly higher than the $240.05 result from mere annual compounding.

That may not seem at first like a big difference, but the end result from quarterly compounding is 2.35% higher than the end result from annual compounding in this example. Now naturally that would make more of a difference if we started with a larger investment than $50.

If we started with $1 million instead of $50, for example, the difference between quarterly compounding and annual compounding over 40 years would amount to $112,805.72 more from quarterly compounding in the end, which—when put in those terms—seems like a lot to me.

Compounding Negative Effects of High Interest Credit Card Debt

Let's try another look at more-frequent-than-annual compounding, with an example from a topic near and dear ("dear" in the sense of costly) to many of our hearts and wallets.

The underlying lesson of this example is how credit card companies can make an extraordinary return on their money lending to us at high interest rates.

We all must pay credit card interest and principal monthly.

Conveniently, for both us and our friendly high-interest credit card lender, minimum payments consist mostly of monthly interest. We hardly get asked to pay back principal at all.

This convenience turns out to be very profitable indeed for our friendly high-interest credit card lender.

In this example I calculate just how profitable—using the compound interest formula with monthly compounding—a $10,000 credit card balance can be at 18% interest. Let's assume I've decided to go on an awesome blowout vacation to Tahiti, and I'll charge the $10,000 cost on my card.

A few clarifying assumptions in the fine print of this example, so that the math stays legit:

1. I assume, overly simply, that we would pay interest only on our monthly bill. In real life, we are typically required to make at least some principal payment.

2. The 18% interest rate will be lower than the legal maximum of 29.99%, but higher than some, more attractive, rates. Even folks with marginal credit scores and high interest cards often have blended rates on their entire credit card obligations, through some low "teaser" rates. The results of this calculation would be more dramatic if I assumed 25% annual or 29% annual interest charges.

3. I'm calculating return on investment for the credit card company, assuming the credit card lender can continuously relend to other borrowers at the assumed rate of 18%. This "cost of money over 10 years" is not the individual borrower's total cost, but rather the credit card lender's "total return" on capital.

4. I'm not accounting for lenders' cost of servicing and marketing, or credit losses due to nonpayment, or other complications of the real world. I'm just showing how a credit card lender can grow its money that it lends to us, through monthly compound interest return.

5. Assume we have the full $10,000 debt outstanding for 10 years, at which point we pay it all off in one sudden payment. (Imagine Uncle Bob dies, with no heirs except us, leaving us a $10,000 legacy. Tragic, but the good news is that we became debt-free!)

Phew, OK, we've gotten the fine-print assumptions out of the way.

Let's start with a present value of personal credit card debt (PV) of $10,000.

We've assumed a yield (Y) of 18%. On a monthly basis—because that's how frequently we have to pay interest—we know that our Y will have be 1.5% (because an 18% annual rate, divided by 12 monthly payments, is 1.5%, but you knew that already).

We can see how that money grows for the credit card company over 10 years, as the lender reinvests our credit card monthly interest payments in other people's credit card loans. We know the number of compounding periods (N) will be 120, because that's the number of payments every month for 10 years.

Returning to our compound interest formula, we can see that the future value (FV) will be, as always, PV * (1 + Y/p)^N.

The future value of the credit card lender's original $10,000, as we pay monthly for 10 years, grows to $10,000 * (1 + 0.015)^120.

Plugging those numbers into my spreadsheet, I get $59,693, or nearly 6 times my initial credit card debt amount. I don't know about you, but that seems like a lot.

Under the assumptions I made above, we will have paid $18,000 in interest, in addition to the original $10,000. Seen that way, we pay a total of $28,000 on the $10,000 credit card debt, or 2.8 times our money. That's also a lot.

But from the credit card company's perspective, reinvesting our interest payments in 18% annual yielding high-interest credit card debt, our original loan can be worth to them 6 times our original amount. That trip to Tahiti cost me a lot more than it seems.

So—just in case you were wondering—that's the math behind why they want you to transfer your balance over to them for an initial low, low, teaser rate!

CHAPTER FIVE

On Discounting Cashflows

After compound interest, discounting cashflows is the most important skill that every financially fit person *should* know, but doesn't know.

Oddly, discounting cashflows never, ever, gets taught in schools. The math is junior high–level math, so I would think high school and college students could be required to master the use of this powerful skill.

This ain't calculus. It's *way* easier. And it's way more useful in your life.

Why Is This Not Taught?

I've thought for a long time about what could be the reasons for never teaching discounted cashflows to high school students.

Is it because Super Evil Mega Corp Conglomerate (the one that secretly controls everything, including the company you bought this book from) does not want people to understand how investing actually works, so they hide this information in a giant conspiracy of ignorance intended to keep the rich wealthy and the poor as impoverished sheeple? Maybe, yes?

I mean, no, not really.

But if it's helpful to think of the silence around discounted cashflows as a secret conspiracy that you can discover and undo by reading this chapter, then go ahead and use that as motivation.

Is it because high school teachers—and the vast majority of college professors—have zero idea how investing works? In part, probably, yes.

Perhaps the cone of silence exists because discounting cashflows is just too complicated for the average educated person to grasp? NO!

That's the point of this chapter. This is not too complicated. Be *optimistic* that you can understand this stuff. Be *skeptical* of the way the investment world presents its seemingly sophisticated face, when underlying it all is this pretty simple math.

Finally, is it because maybe I'm wrong, and discounting cashflows is not an essential skill? No. I am not wrong.

This is the *fundamental skill* used to invest money. Now, you may not want to invest money for a living, and frankly I don't blame you in the least for that choice. But in that case you will need to make certain financial choices that involve someone else investing for you, such as your bank, your government, your insurance company, and your broker. And you want to know the whats, whys, and hows with your money. Your ability to understand the skill behind investing can open up a whole world of understanding about what it is that the person you hired is actually doing.

Learning the Math

It's not hard, and if you've learned compound interest, then it's kind of a snap.

But it does involve math and poking around with a spreadsheet.

Just like the last chapter on compound interest, you should *definitely* open up a spreadsheet as you read through this chapter, as it's the only way to actually learn how to discount cashflows yourself.

So What Is It?

Discounting cashflows—in the simplest mathematical sense—is just the opposite action to compound interest.

I mean opposite in the way that subtraction is the opposite action of addition and division is the opposite action of multiplication. And—for that matter—square roots are the opposite of raised-to-the-power-of exponents.

In that same sense, discounting cashflows is the opposite of compound interest.

And just like the compound interest formula showed us how the mathematical bridge of interest rates and time connects today's money to future money, the discounted cashflows formula showed us the same bridge, only in reverse. We connect future money to a value of money today.

Calculating compound interest, you recall from the last chapter, tells us precisely how money (or kittens, or snowballs) grows from a certain known amount today (PV) into a known amount in the future (FV), through the intervention of an interest rate (Y) and multiple compounding periods (N).

The formula we learned in the previous chapter on compound interest is $FV = PV * (1 + Y)^N$.

Again, that's how a known amount of feral kittens today (PV) becomes a predictably known amount of kittens in the future (FV) through a growth rate (Y) and a number of compounding periods (N). (And a lot of kitty litter along the way.)

Discounting cashflows moves in the opposite direction. We move backward in time, from the future back to the present.

Specifically, the discounting cashflows formula tells us how a certain known amount of money in the future (FV) can be "discounted" back to a certain known amount in the present (FV) through the intervention of an interest rate (Y) and multiple compounding periods (N).

Notice that we use the exact same variables in both formulas. Notice, also, that the only difference mathematically is that we're solving for a different number.

The discounted cashflow formula simply reverses the algebra of the compound interest formula.

The discounted cashflow formula solves for present value, so that:

$$PV = FV / (1 + Y)^N$$

If you remember your algebra skills, you will see that this is the exact same formula as compound interest, except that instead of "solving for" or isolating FV, we've "solved for" and isolated PV.

So why do we care about discounting cashflows?

Discounting cashflows is the basis for *all* investing. Full stop. Punto. End of story.

It allows us to estimate the present value, or in plainer language—how much we would pay today for a future amount of money.

And notice that's exactly what we're doing when we invest money. We pay for, or invest, some amount of money today, in order to get a larger amount of money returned, some time in the future. The discounted cashflows formula tells us how much we should pay for that future money. How much is that future money worth to me today? That's what I'll pay. That's investing.

Example 1: An Inheritance

A simplified example should help to get us started, then later in the chapter—and in the Appendix—we'll tackle some further examples to solidify our understanding.

How much would an inheritance coming in 5 years be worth, today?

If I know for example I'm set to inherit $5,000 from my uncle 5 years from now, what would that be worth to me today, like, right now? I know we don't "pay" for an inheritance, but you can think of it as "How much would I pay today to get $5,000 in 5 years?"

If I assume a certain interest rate or yield—also known in this context as a "discount rate" but mathematically it represents the same exact thing—I can calculate the worth to me today of the future $5,000.

By the way, again, if you want to start to learn this formula for real, open up a spreadsheet right now and let's calculate the answer. Simply reading the words here will not suffice. Nor for that matter will "cheating" and using a financial calculator, because that's not a flexible enough tool—in my opinion—for solving any discounted cashflow situation you could encounter in your real life. You have to actually follow along with the mathematics using a spreadsheet. Just trust me on this one.

OK, back to our inheritance. Are you excited? I'm excited for this.

We know the FV is $5,000, the amount we expect in the future.

We know the N is 5, for 5 years' worth of discounting.

PV, the present value of the future inheritance, is what we're solving for with the formula.

So what's Y?

Let's assume for the moment a 4% Y, or discount rate. (More on that assumed Y in a moment, just below the math solution.)

If Y is 4%, then the math involves just plugging in numbers for FV, N, and Y into the discounted cashflows formula, which we remember from above is

$$PV = FV / (1+Y)^N$$

(I implore you—once more—to open up a spreadsheet here and create a simple spreadsheet formula to solve this math. Doing it by hand, or even with a financial calculator, just isn't efficient or robust enough.)

So, PV (what we're trying to solve for) is equal to $5,000 / (1+0.04)^5

That's easy-peasy math for your spreadsheet formula.

The present value is $5,000 / 1.216653.

Or $4,110 rounded to the nearest dollar.

In investment terms, that means we should be willing to pay $4,110 today in order to receive $5,000 in inheritance, 5 years from now. Again, we don't really pay for an inheritance, but the example is meant to show what that future inheritance is worth today, 5 years in advance of payment.

By the Way, How Did I Come Up with 4%?

Frankly and honestly, I made up the 4% for the example.

I don't just say I made it up to be flippant. I mean to emphasize that I made it up because making up Y, or the proper yield or discount rate (remember, those mean the same thing!) is a key to effectively using the discounted cashflows formula.

In fact, any time you discount cashflows, you have to "make up," or assume, a certain Y or discount rate, and the Y assumption you use is as much art as science.

Is that 4% Y I assumed correct?

I don't know, but it's reasonable, and that's usually the most we can say about any assumed Y. How do we come up with a reasonable Y number?

Y as an interest rate or discount rate (remember: same thing!) reflects a combination of:

1.   the market cost of money, which is often called an interest rate,
2.   the expectation of inflation in the future, and
3.   the risk of the payment actually being made in the future.

Only some of these things can be known at any time, so only some of our Y is scientifically knowable. The rest has to be assumed according to best estimates. That's why we can reasonably say that sometimes this Y assumption is as much art as science.

The rest of this chapter—after the following caveat—will provide examples of how we use discounted cashflows in real-life investing.

Do You Have to Learn This?

Can you do just fine without learning how to discount cashflows? Yes.

Do 999 out of 1,000 people know how to do this? No.

And it turns out many of those 999 people out of 1,000 do just fine in life. They have friends. They seem normal and well adjusted. Some of them even grow wealthy. They remain ignorant of the importance and usefulness of discounting cashflows, but they get by OK in life. All true.

But I want to mention three reasons to learn this skill.

First, most generally, getting wealthy may involve learning things that others haven't bothered to learn or haven't been able to learn. Being different is to your advantage here.

Second, all investing, properly understood, is based fundamentally on discounting cashflows. Seriously, all investing!

That statement probably sounds weird because, as I mentioned already, 999 out of 1,000 people don't know how to do this. Yet many more people than 1 in a 1,000 believe they are "investing," without knowing this technique. Which means they "invest"—in an important sense—blind.

Or they are doing something different than investing, such as guessing, or speculating, or fingers-crossing, or something else. I don't know what.

Third, even if you never invest yourself—even if you hire a fund manager or investment adviser to do this for you—you should understand discounting cashflows. Knowing the math of discounting cashflows is going to help you judge the extent to which the people you hired know what they are doing.

Here's a scary yet true statement: the vast majority of investment advisers—certainly a vast majority of financial salespeople masquerading as investment advisers—do not know how to discount cashflows. Which means you should consider firing them and hiring yourself![1]

Or something.

I mean, don't really fire them right away, because even these financial sales-people may be able to help you in other ways, as we'll discuss in Chapter 15. Just not, probably, as experts on investing.

OK, what I really mean is this: discounting cashflows is the basis for *all* investing. If you mastered the technique, and then realized how little this fundamental skill is understood by the people you pay to help you, you will:

1.   Become *optimistic* that you'll know more about finance than most of the so-called experts, and many more things could be done by you, yourself, than you originally thought. This will tend to save you money.

2.   Develop a healthy *skepticism* about what the experts are selling.

3.   Adopt a *modest* attitude toward how much fundamental investing you need to do yourself.

Application to Business Owners

This may seem like a tangent, and more related to the section of Chapter 21 about entrepreneurship, but the ability to calculate discounted cash-flows does more than just make you literate in investing. That skill is also the financial basis of good decision making when it comes to business growth, business investment, and merger activities.

You see, the decision to pay for something today in order to receive cash-flows in the future is what an entrepreneur or CEO has to make.

Should I buy this company? Well, a key piece of information is whether the future cashflows, discounted back to the present, justify the cost today.

Should I build out this new product line? Well, what are the future cash-flows you can estimate based on that product? When you discount them back to the present, are they more or less than what you need to pay today?

In the Appendix for this chapter I discuss the use of discounted cashflow analysis for deciding which price to accept when selling a business.

---

[1] If you have an investment adviser, or if you are considering hiring one, try out the test above on your person. Say, "I'm going to inherit $5,000 in exactly 5 years. Assuming a 4% discount rate, what is the precise present value of that inheritance, today?" I wonder how many of your candidates will know to plug in $5,000 / (1 + 0.04)^5 to a spreadsheet or their calculator to get $4,110? Possibly very few.

Application to Policy Makers

When our elected officials agree to pay long-term public pensions to retirees, calculating discounted cashflows is how we figure out the cost in today's dollars. When a retiree elects to receive a $50,000 pension for the next 24 years, we can know precisely what that is worth, if we apply a discount rate to each of those $50,000 payments.

OK, now, if you open up a fresh spreadsheet, you really can master the discounted cashflows formula using this chapter, and the Chapter 5 Appendix, with a little patience and practice.

Example 2: Single Lump Sum Like an Annuity Payout

Let's start simple, spreadsheet open.

A builder's insurance company offers you a $25,000 lump sum payment to compensate you for the pain and hardship of an injured pet hit by an errant beam that fell from his construction site.

Picture a big piece of wood that hurt the dog's paw. The dog will likely make a full recovery, but the developer/builder offered you this settlement to avoid a costly lawsuit with bad public relations potential.

Importantly, however, the settlement will be paid out 10 years from now. Note, by the way, that this is common practice in injury-settlement cases.

Lump sums get offered far into the future. This is partly because such agreements incentivize the victim/beneficiary to comply with the terms of the settlement for the longest period of time. But also importantly, as we will see, it's much cheaper for the insurance company to make payments deep into the future.

Now, back to the math.

Let's assume the insurance company is a very safe, stable company, and we expect moderate inflation, so the proper Y, or discount rate for the next 10 years, is around 3%.

How much is that settlement worth to us today?

Let's go to the spreadsheet.

We set up our formula in a spreadsheet that the value today, or present value (PV), is equal to FV / (1 + Y)^N.

We know the future payout, FV, is $25,000.

We know how many years we have to wait, so N is 10.

We've assumed a Y of 3%.

The present value will be equal to $25,000 / (1 + 3%)^10.

This is easy-peasy math for your spreadsheet, which tells us the present value is $18,602, rounded to the nearest dollar.

What does this mean in practice? We're not going to invest $18,602 in this future $25,000 insurance payout, but it can be very helpful for us to understand that the future $25,000 payment really only costs the insurance company about 75% of what it first appears to cost.

Incidentally, using discounted cashflows can give us extraordinary insight into how an insurance company operates, and how it makes money. In a related story—as we'll discuss in Chapter 16, "On Insurance"—you don't want to buy too much insurance.

If you'd like to do more discounted cashflows practice before moving on to Chapter 6, I recommend turning to the following Appendix to get further practice on this essential investing technique.

Appendix

This Appendix makes the most sense after reading Chapter 5 on discounting cashflows and working through that math.

If you'd enjoy a deeper dive using video and watching me walk through some discounted cashflows examples, I encourage you to visit my website:

http://www.bankers-anonymous.com/blog/discounted-cashflows-deeper -dive

This section gets us closer to how discounting cashflows math gets used in real life, by actual banks, insurance companies, entrepreneurs, and bond and stock investors. I want to warn you upfront that there's some math here. Many of you may be turned off by math. The first thing I'll say about your aversion is that you can absolutely do great in life without using this math, and Chapters 6 through 21 do not require you to be able to do this on your own.

The second thing I'll say is that I passionately believe that many more people can and should learn this, as it can change your financial life. Third, it drives me crazy that personal finance books for a general audience never bother to teach this the right way.

Many finance books that try to teach the fundamentals of discounting cashflows and bond investing make use of a discounted cashflows table, to which readers can refer, to figure out the present value of future bond payments. But these tables are a terrible idea. First, following the widespread use of computers, nobody in the real investment world after say, 1982, would ever refer to a discounted cashflows table to value a bond. And yet, that method keeps showing up in books.

At this point, with spreadsheets available to all, tables in books should be banned as a method for discounting cashflows. Anyway, that's a pet peeve of mine. So I want you to learn this the right way.

One more throat-clearing note before we plunge into the math. The examples to follow are how an entrepreneur selling a business, a bond investor, and a stock investor would use discounting cashflows to determine financial value. To work up to this, you should already master the Examples 1 and 2 from this chapter. If you take your time with those examples, you will be ready to tackle these examples.

The examples below apply specifically as follows:

Example 3: Entrepreneur

Example 4: Bond Investor

Example 5: Stock Investor

If you'd like to learn this for real, just like for Examples 1 and 2, I recommend taking your time, with a spreadsheet open, to follow along each step. The math does not go beyond early high school skills, but is not "intuitive" without literally working through the examples on the spreadsheet. If you do master these skills, I optimistically propose you'll have a better intuition about how the financial world around us works.

Example 3: Multiple Annual Future Payments—Entrepreneur Selling a Business

Let's add a little complexity over the earlier Chapter 5 examples by adding in multiple future payments for which we need to calculate a present value.

Let's assume you are ready to retire, and you plan to sell a business you own. The business purchasers agree to pay you $300,000 for your business. But instead of offering all that money now, they plan to pay you in annual installments of $30,000, each and every year for the next 10 years.

You're tempted, but you want to know, what is this payout really worth today?

We can even think about a scenario in which you have a competing offer of $200,000 for your business, with all the cash paid to you upfront, this year.

To calculate the worth of 10 future payments, we need to discount those payments to the present day, which we can then compare to the $200,000 all-cash offer.

Let's assume the business you plan to sell is somewhat risky, making those 10 future pension payments also somewhat risky. The right discount rate (or Y) is something like 12% annually.

[About that 12% Y assumption: please know that the 12% discount rate (Y) is really an assumption based on as much art as science. If my business is somewhat risky, I might base my discount rate on comparable "junk bond" interest rates for other risky companies. I could also take into account prevailing interest rates of the economy, as well as inflation expectations. Is 12%

the right discount rate? I don't know, but I can start with that and change it later. If you program the formula into your spreadsheet correctly, changing the Y just takes a moment.]

Now we can calculate each of the annual payments separately.

Let's start with the furthest-in-the-future payment of $30,000.

The payment 10 years from now will have a future value (FV) = $30,000, a discount rate (Y) of 12%, and the number of years (N) is 10. Plugging those numbers into our present value formula of PV = FV / (1 + Y)^N, we get $30,000 / (1 + 12%)^10, which my spreadsheet tells me is equal to $9,659.

Now how about the next-furthest-away payment?

The payment due 9 years from now will have a FV of $30,000, a Y of 12%, and an N of 9.

Plugging that into the formula PV = FV / (1 + Y)^N we get $30,000 / (1 + 12%)^9. My spreadsheet produces a present value for this payment of $10,818.

I follow this process for all 10 separate annual payments—in fact this all takes about 8 seconds if you can do an auto-fill on your spreadsheet—and I add up all 10 annual payments to arrive at a value of $169,507, rounded to the nearest dollar.

This is a lot less than the $300,000 headline offer I thought I was getting at first glance.

Is That a Good Deal or Not?

That depends.[2]

At least now we have a way of comparing the 10-year installment payout offer versus another offer that might be for the entire company in one single payment.

If somebody offers $200,000 today, versus the $300,000 in 10 annual installments, a good case could be made that $200,000 today is worth more.

If you've got the discounting formulas set up on your spreadsheet, you can see that the comparison depends on what discount rate, or Y, you assume those 10 future payments deserve.

When I play around with assumptions on my spreadsheet, I see that an 8% discount rate makes the 10-year payout of $300,000 roughly equal to $200,000 today. If the payments are not very risky, or inflation stays low, 8% might be a fair discount rate. Again, this is a judgment call involving art as well as science. But the formula helps us look at those different scenarios, comparing money today versus multiple future payments.

---

[2]I'm skipping the issue of whether there are tax differences between being paid money upfront and receiving installment payments. Taxes are important—although as I emphasize in Chapter 10, "On Taxes," not too important. For the moment, we're trying to simplify for the sake of understanding the math, so we disregard the taxes to focus on the math theory.

Intuition Around Y, and Using Y to Help Your Intuition

At this point, using this example, it may be worth pausing to reflect again on the concept of Y, or discount rate.

Remember that the assumed Y takes into account a combination of three factors: prevailing interest rates, inflation expectations, and the risk of the future payments themselves. Some of this is not knowable, meaning Y must always be a "best guess" combination of art and science.

If you've got 10 future payments from our example programmed into your spreadsheet, all linked to the same discount rate (your Y value), you can use your spreadsheet to give you intuition around the effect of changing risk assumptions.

I mean by that the following. If your business is very risky, we would apply a very high discount rate to all future payments from the business.

Maybe 20%? Your spreadsheet will spit out a value of $125,774 for the sum of 10 years' worth of $30,000 payments, discounted at a 20% rate.

Maybe 25%? Your spreadsheet will spit out a value of $107,115 for the sum of 10 years' worth of $30,000 payments discounted at a 25% rate.

If you know your business is highly risky as you look to sell, you will intuitively know to take the $200,000 cash upfront, rather than wait a long time for $300,000 in cash. The discounted cashflows formula helps you put a mathematical value on that intuition, using a numerical representation of that risk. The numerical representation of that risk, again, is the variable Y.

To go in the other direction, maybe the future cashflows of your business, by contrast, are very safe? Maybe you only apply a 5% discount rate? Well then, the sum of all those future payments are worth $231,652 today, according to my spreadsheet. Take the long payout, because that's worth more than the $200,000 all-cash offer. With a safe series of cashflows, you'll have intuition that a long payout is OK. With the discounted cashflows formula, again, you can put a mathematical value today on that intuition. You begin to think and act like a fundamental investor.

More Complex Examples. The next few examples add yet another layer of complexity, but also get us even closer to how the discounted cashflows formula gets used in practice by investors, insurance companies, and banks.

Example 4: Multiple Future Cashflows, at Semiannual Intervals, Like a Bond

People who buy bonds, bond investors, are putting up money today in order to receive a series of future payments. Determining how much money a bond investor would pay for those future payments is the number one skill of a professional bond investor.

Bond investors use the discounted cashflows formula as the fundamental tool of their trade. With it, bond investors take each individual cashflow of a bond, discount it back to its present value, and add up all the different present values. The sum of all the present values matters because it's how much any investor would pay for a bond.

Wall Street wizards in all their glorious mathematical ingenuity have come up with an infinite variety of bond types. In the interest of simplicity, however, we are not going to describe this delightful variety. I'm going to describe below the most boring animal in the bond zoo: a semiannual, fixed rate, "bullet" bond. It does not amortize, that is to say, pay off principal early. It does not have a floating interest rate. It pays all principal upon maturity. This is what we'd call a "plain-vanilla" bond, for those of you who enjoy ice cream metaphors.

Cashflows That Come More Frequently Than Annually
A typical bond pays investors semiannually, meaning two payments per year. Those semiannual payments will be one-half of the stated fixed interest rate—or coupon—of the bond.

So if we look to evaluate a 4% bond, then we would expect two payments per year, each consisting of 2% of the bond principal. I get to 2% because 2% is half of the stated 4% interest rate, but you knew that already.

If the stated fixed interest rate were 12%, we would expect two semiannual payments of 6%. If the stated fixed interest rate were 7%, we would expect two semiannual payments of 3.5%. By now most likely you are seeing the pattern.

You may be wondering, quite rightly, how much money gets paid by a bond, when stated in percent terms. I wrote "2% semiannual payment," but you're possibly thinking "2% of what?"

Good question.

The 2% (or whatever percent payment) is a percentage of the original principal of the bond.

Oh yeah, sorry, I forgot to mention: bonds (the plain-vanilla ones, anyway) always have a fixed amount of principal. This is also known as the face amount of the bond. This amount always has to be repaid at the end of the life of the bond, also known as the "maturity" of the bond.

The semiannual coupon is calculated as a percentage of the face amount.

So, for example, on my $1,000,000 bond, a 2% semiannual coupon will be $20,000, because that's 2% of $1,000,000. Here are more examples so that the math sinks in. A 5% coupon on a $5,000,000 bond would be $250,000, because that's 5% of $5,000,000. A 7% coupon on a $100,000 bond would be $7,000, because that's 7% of $100,000. A 2.75% coupon on a $50,000 bond would be $1,375, because that's 2.75% of $50,000. Again, by now you are most likely seeing the pattern.

As I mentioned above, the typical bond has a set principal payment that gets paid at the end, or maturity, of a bond. A typical 3-year bond, therefore, makes six semiannual coupon payments and then a final principal repayment at the end of 3 years.

To continue with our hypothetical $1,000,000 bond with a 4% interest rate, the payments would look like this:

6 months—$20,000

12 months—$20,000

18 months—$20,000

24 months—$20,000

30 months—$20,000

36 months—$20,000 + $1,000,000

To value a bond—to fully calculate its present value—we need to add up all of the separate present values of the interim coupon payments, plus the present value of the final maturity payment.

That means we take each cashflow made at different future time intervals, apply a discount specific to that time interval, and then add up all the present values to get a single value for the bond. This may sound complex when written out in words, but the use of a spreadsheet makes all this math pretty straightforward, as explained in the following section.

Calculating Six Present Values

Let's take these bond cashflows one at a time, starting with the first $20,000 cashflow, due in 6 months. This is the point where you absolutely have to open up a spreadsheet for the following bit to make any sense at all. Otherwise you'll just be reading my word salad jibberish. OK, deal?

We know the future value (FV) of the payment is $20,000.

For six regular payments at regular intervals, we can assign an N of one through six to each of the six future payments. For the first $20,000 due in 6 months, we can use an N of 1.

The discount rate (Y) requires us to mix a little artistic judgment to our financial science. Let's say I expect the bond to be quite safe, and inflation to be low, so I will apply a 3% annual discount rate to the bond payments.

Really you can, and should, try applying different discount rates (Y) to these future payments. The best way to understand discounting cashflows is to model up future bond payments and insert different discount rates, and see how the present values change. This, again, is the fundamental task of professional bond investing. On this particular bond, if you use a 4% discount rate on all of the future bond cashflows, the value will be exactly $1,000,000. If you use a 5% discount rate, the present value will be less than $1,000,000. This is how some bonds can be worth less than their original principal amount (applying a high discount rate, or yield), while other bonds can be worth more than their original principal amount (applying a low discount rate, or yield).

Adjusting Y for Semiannual Payments

Up until this example, we have used Y as an annual discount rate.

In this example, however, before we calculate the present value of our first payment, we have to make an additional adjustment for the discount rate of the payment, because it's not made at an annual interval.

Because we usually discuss discount rates in annual terms, we can accurately say we will apply a 3% annual discount rate.

For a payment made in 6 months, however, we have to apply a discount rate that's been adjusted for semiannual payments.

We always do this by dividing our discount rate (Y) by the number of payments being made in a year, or the variable P.

In this case, for example, two semiannual payments require us to divide our 3% Y by 2. If we worked with quarterly payments we would have to divide our annual-rate Y by 4.

A few more examples may help set the pattern. If we analyzed payments made monthly, we would divide Y by 12. If we analyzed payments made six times per year, we would divide Y by 6. By now you are probably getting the pattern.

Applying a 3% annual discount rate to my bond cashflows, therefore, requires me to input 1.5% as my adjusted Y in my spreadsheet.

For payments made more frequently than annually, you can elect to follow the pattern I've set above, which is adjust Y by dividing your annual Y by the number of payments per year. Or, to get the same result, you can introduce a variable p in your discounted cashflows formula, in which p represents the number of payments made per year, and the formula could be updated to $PV = FV / (1 + Y/p)^{\wedge}N$.

Back to the First Coupon Payment

All right, so, now we can input in our spreadsheet the proper values to figure out the present value of our first coupon.

We know present value of the first coupon $(PV) = FV / (1 + Y/p)^{\wedge}N$, so I program my spreadsheet to tell me the dollar value today of $20,000 / (1 + 1.5\%)^{\wedge}1$.

My handy spreadsheet tells me that's worth $19,704, rounded to the nearest dollar.

The Rest of the Payments

Next, I program my spreadsheet to tell me the dollar value today (PV) of the second coupon. Notice that as we've moved away from annual discounting to semiannual discounting, the variable N is no longer number of years, but rather number of discounting periods.

The N of my second time period is 2, so my PV formula must be $20,000 / (1 + 1.5\%)^2$. My handy spreadsheet spits out a value for me of $19,413, rounded to the nearest dollar.

So far, so good. Same method, third coupon, $20,000 / (1 + 1.5\%)^3$, gets me a present value of $19,126, rounded to the nearest dollar.

Remaining payments on my spreadsheet look like this:

Payment 4: $=\$20,000 / (1 + 1.5\%)^4 = \$18,844$

Payment 5: $=\$20,000 / (1 + 1.5\%)^5 = \$18,565$

Payment 6: $= \$1,020,000 / (1 + 1.5\%)^6 = \$932,833$

Remember to notice that Payment 6 is a combination of the sixth coupon payment and the return of the original principal of $1,000,000, as is typical of a plain-vanilla bond.

When you add those all up, you get a value of $1,028,486, rounded to the nearest dollar.

In plain language, a bond investor seeking a 3% yield from this bond would be willing to pay $1,028,486. The price a bond buyer is willing to pay flows directly from the discount rate he or she applies to all future bond cashflows. In the bond investing world yield, or discount rate, is the most important choice an investor makes. The price, or present value, flows mathematically from the choice about yield.

A Bit More on Bond Pricing, Probably More Than You Really Want to Know

In the bond world, professionals quote bond prices as a percentage of 100%, so they might refer to this bond above as a bond priced at 102.8486 or—to further confuse outsiders[3]—the professionals might quote this in fractional terms, such as 102 and 27/32nds, which is a roughly, but not precisely, accurate price.

Now, if that same bond investor sought to earn a 5% annual yield, the bond investor would need to update this annual Y to 5, and an adjusted Y/p of 2.5% applied to each semiannual cashflow in the spreadsheet. If you've built your

---

[3]It's not really to confuse outsiders, but rather is a historical convention of the bond market to use fractions for pricing rather than decimals. The larger the size of the bond and the more efficient the bond market pricing, the more likely the price would be decimalized rather than fractionalized. But, whatever.

spreadsheet formulas already, you can see how switching Y/p to 2.5% changes all of the present values immediately.

The new value of a 4% coupon bond shifts to $972,459, or 97.2459, or maybe just 97¼ for short.

Example 5: Discounting Multiple Future Cashflows at Quarterly Intervals, Like a Stock

Investing in stocks, for the fundamental investor, is really just the purchase in today's dollars of future cashflows, in the form of profits, if any, and dividends, if any. In that sense, the skill of fundamental stock investing is to discount the value of all future cashflows into present values. The sum of all these cashflows then becomes the price at which you should pay for a stock.

The Example of a Risky Stock

Let's say we were looking at buying stock in a particularly risky company. It's so risky, in fact, that we should apply a 35% discount rate to all future cashflows. With our limited amount of funds, we can purchase one millionth of the company, which coincidentally (to keep our math kind of simple) produces precisely 4 million dollars in profits a year, or 1 million dollars per quarter of a year.

As a purchaser of one millionth of the company, we would be buying $4 of profit per year, or $1 in profit per quarter.

OK, that's the setup. How much is our stock worth?

Admittedly I've created a simple scenario, but one I hope will illustrate how fundamental stock investing can work. Because given all the information I've provided, we can know the fundamental value of this stock precisely!

In one quarter of a year from now, with our stock purchase, we will in essence "own" a $1 cashflow, in the form of our one millionth ownership of this risky company's profits.

How much is that $1 worth, discounted by 35%, for one quarter? Easy-peasy, with our discounted cashflow formula:

We have future cashflow (PV) of $1.

We have a discount rate (Y) of 35%.

We have a number of periods in the year (p) of 4, since we're counting quarterly profits.

And we are looking at the first period (N), which is one quarter from now.

I calculate this cashflow as $1 / (1 + 35\% / 4)^1$.

I plug that into my spreadsheet and find out that it equals $0.92.

I can then repeat the process for the next few quarters and then the next few years' worth of $1 cashflow profits, which in my spreadsheet is the matter of about 8 seconds' worth of work using the auto-fill function.

Quarter 2 profits will be $1 / (1 + 35\% / 4)^2$—which is equal to $0.85

Quarter 3 profits will be $1 / (1 + 35\% / 4)^3$—which is equal to $0.78

Quarter 4 profits will be $1 / (1 + 35\% / 4)^4$—which is equal to $0.71

I can continue to calculate each future cashflow separately, and then add them all up in my spreadsheet.

Adding up the next 20 quarters, or 5 years' worth of profits, I get a value of $9.29. If I extend my spreadsheet out to say, 50 years' worth of future $1 quarterly profits, the total value of all the discounted cashflows is $11.43.

When I do that, I can say that the stock is fundamentally worth $11.43.

This is super-useful to know, because if the stock trades at something less than $11.43, I could reasonably argue that on a fundamental basis, the stock is cheap. If the stock trades at something higher than $11.43, I could reasonably argue that the stock is expensive. This, right here, is exactly what all fundamental stock investing attempts to do. You model up all the future cashflows of a business, then discount cashflows to the present day, and add them all up. The sum of all the cashflows is the fundamental value, today, of that business.

Interestingly, with a 35% discount rate, I only need to extend my calculations to about 15 years before the value of each quarterly $1 future profit shrinks to an infinitesimally small size, a size that no longer affects the present value of the company. In plain terms, for a highly risky company with a 35% discount rate applied to its profits, the far-out future (beyond 15 years) doesn't matter all that much. For safer companies, with lower discount rates, far-out future years matter more to fundamental value.

A Few Observations of Fundamental Investing

Although I've kept the example extremely simple, I hope this bit of math above explains a few phenomena of fundamental stock investing. For example:

- Profits of companies perceived as less risky (like utilities, for example) are worth more to fundamental investors—because mathematically you apply a lower discount rate to its future cashflows. Similarly, nonvolatile profits are worth more to investors because they are also mathematically easier to predict, reflected in a lower discount rate.
- Start-up companies without known profits, or in swiftly changing, risky, businesses are less valuable, because fundamental investors apply high discount rates to any modeling of future cashflows.

This discounting of future profits of a stock explained above is the basis for what's known as fundamental or "value" investing. The godfather of this approach is Benjamin Graham (and his more-famous disciple, Warren Buffett), and I recommend Graham's book *The Intelligent Investor* for more on the use of discounted cashflows to invest this way.

Buffett famously rejected investing in volatile technology-based businesses, presumably because he found it too difficult to accurately discount future, unknowable, cashflows.

And Now, for the Unfortunate Reality of Stock Investing

In real-life investing, unfortunately, all the information is not as clear and unambiguous as I've presented it in the above example.

We generally wouldn't really know, for example, that a company will produce profits, like clockwork, of $1 per quarter. Profits could go down or profits could go up, complicating our calculations. The imprecise nature of modeling future profits means fundamental investing is not as mathematically precise as it at first appears.

Similarly, we don't really know if 35% is the right discount rate to apply to future quarterly profits.

If the company for some reason became less risky, and I could reasonably apply a more generous discount rate like 25% to reflect that decline in risk, suddenly the sum of present values of future cashflows jumps to $16, and we need to consider up to 25 years, or even more, worth of future quarterly profits in our calculation.

I have two other, seemingly contradictory thoughts, on this idea. I hope that the fact that they are contradictory is not too off-putting. The world, including the investment world, is a complex, sometime contradictory, place. The following two contradictory truths are one example of this complexity.

First, anyone who is NOT discounting cashflows like this is—in some fundamental way—not actually investing. They are gambling, or guessing, or counting on the "greater fool" theory, or praying, or punting, or whatever. The greater fool theory incidentally is the idea of buying something in the hopes that it will go up in price, purchased by a greater fool than me, so I can make a profit.

Second—and here's the contradictory idea—applying the correct discount rate *and* correctly assuming future cashflows in fact requires a tremendous amount of guesswork about fundamentally unknowable future events.

So even if you're doing everything "correctly" the way Benjamin Graham and Warren Buffett would advocate, you're still in a way gambling or guessing or praying or punting or whatever. How can anyone really know what the profits of any company will look like in 5 years? You can't know. So frustrating.

I don't say this to endorse gambling and praying and punting with your money, but rather to introduce an essential *modesty* about how much anyone can actually know about future unknowable things.

What I mean is this: the more certain the rocket-scientist financial modeler seems—even one properly discounting cashflows—the more *skeptical* we need to be to counteract that certainty.

This ends the Appendix on discounting future cashflows, which I hope has given some insight into how this skill is the fundamental basis for all legitimate investing activity. You don't *have* to understand this to be financially savvy, but I hope you will be left with the following ideas.

Be *skeptical* of complicated-seeming investment presentations. At base, all of it comes down to variations on this chapter's math.

Be *optimistic* that with a little bit of practice and some time, you could do all the math required for fundamental investing.

Understanding how much time and effort it could take to actually come up with the correct estimate of future cashflows, plus their proper discount rate, you might be left feeling *modest* about your own ability to do this better than someone else.

These are all healthy responses to learning about discounting cashflows.

PART 3

Just Starting Out: Getting to Surplus

CHAPTER SIX

On High-Interest Debt

High-interest debt is the easiest thing in the world to acquire—like the common cold, except even easier. Maybe you picked up a free T-shirt at that college welcome fair freshman year and acquired your credit card to go with it. Or you signed up for 50,000 airline mileage points at the airport kiosk. Either card will be charging you 25% interest before you even blink.

As an experiment I once walked into a payday lending shop in my hometown and walked out 25 minutes later with $200 cash. It was so darned easy! Until I paid $50 in interest a month later, or 25% *monthly* interest.

If you walk onto a car lot with little cash and no credit history, maybe you'll get a subprime auto loan for a 13% annual rate.

You don't have any cash for clothes at the dress shop, renovation supplies at the hardware store, or $500 for Fluffy's deworming medicine at the vet? All of these places can provide you with high-interest cards if you'll just sign right here on the line. You might even get $10 off when you sign up!

I'm starting with high-interest debt because the order of presentation in this book matters tremendously to me. First things first, next things next, last things last.

High-interest debt is the first topic for this "starting out" section because if you don't work on this first, nothing else matters. *You cannot build wealth and also maintain high-interest debt balances.* Full stop.

Good News, Bad News

I'll describe the bad news problem with high-interest debt in more detail later in the chapter, but guess what the silver lining to living under a dark cloud of high-interest debt is?

Simplicity!

Dramatically improving your personal financial situation—if you have high-interest debt—remains very, very, simple at this point. Everything you need to know right now about fixing your finances is right here. You don't need to read beyond this page in this chapter. Right now, you can put down this book and just work on your single, simple plan.

Pay down your high-interest debt.

So simple. With high interest debt, you'll never get wealthy. Take care of your high interest debt, however, and you've at least got a fighting chance at building wealth.

So easy, right? Well.

How you do it, as a practical matter, is indeed simple, but far from easy.

We'll talk about some useful techniques in Chapter 7 on saving, and some tax considerations in Chapter 9 on retirement accounts, and Chapter 12 on homeownership. I'll return to those ideas at the end of the chapter to be a bit more nuanced in my advice. But really, you only need to understand one big thing: pay down all high-interest debt to zero.

High-Interest Debt Taxonomy

What are the various kinds of high-interest debt, and how will you know if you have any?

Here's a partial list of mainstream high-interest debts, although high-interest lenders are so darned creative there will be other kinds of expensive loans not mentioned here.

Payday loans: Possibly the most egregious of legal high-interest loans. Structured for just a few weeks to 3 months, the annual interest rates on these advances against your paycheck can reach over 100%.

Pawn shop loans: Collateralized by some valuable item you own, these 60- to 90-day loans can also have an annual rate of over 100% per year.

Car title loans: With high monthly interest and the rights to your car as collateral, these reach above 100% annual rates per year.

Tax advance loans: "Tax preparation" companies help figure out your income tax refund, then lend you the money while you wait for the IRS to send it in the mail, for the equivalent of a very high annual interest rate. They only lend you money for a few weeks to a few months, but the equivalent annual rate will be very high.

Credit card balances: While you may briefly get 0% teaser rates, eventually the companies know the cost of you carrying a monthly balance will approach the average 12% rate. This can easily shoot up to the legally allowable 29.99% annual rate.

Subprime home loans: At many percentage points higher than conventional prime mortgages, this is an expensive way to buy a house. You need to work toward a lower-cost prime loan instead.

Subprime car loans: Many car dealerships are built on profit from selling high-interest car loans more than actually selling cars. Car loans can be very affordable if you have good credit, but many subprime loans are very expensive.

This is only a partial list of the most common and legal ways in which you might be paying way more to borrow money than is compatible with building wealth.

Is All Debt Bad?

Now, nestled in the title of this chapter is a key distinction about personal debt to which I'd like to call your attention.

Notice I'm calling out a difference between high-interest debt and low-interest debt.

I believe deeply in this difference.

In brief:

High-interest debt = not compatible with building wealth.

Low-interest debt = compatible with building wealth.

Not everyone agrees with me on this point.

A popular and well-known personal finance guru, for example, insists that his followers eschew all debts and pay for everything with cash. All debt, he insists, will keep you poor. Any debt, he implores, keeps you from getting wealthy. For him, the best way to buy a car or a house is to save up all the money in cash first. Years later, when you have the money, you can make your purchase.

I disagree with this guru.

Look, he's a little bit right but quite a bit wrong.

He's right that for some people, debt can get out of control. Debt becomes a compulsion and a crutch, and ultimately a crushing weight.

For the recently bankrupt or the perennially broke, all debt hurts.

Debt Is a Drug, for Both Good and Evil

But for many of us, debt is a complex mixture of danger and opportunity. In that sense, debt is a drug. Like prescription pharmaceuticals, debt can be life saving—or at least life enhancing—for some. That same debt drug can be devastating to others. If you've had trouble with the debt drug in the past, you may not be able to handle even a drop, whether of the high- or low-interest variety.

But if you're not susceptible to that particular addiction, low-interest debt can help you achieve many life goals, including especially, wealth building. I return to that theme in Chapter 8.

When do you get stuck with high-interest debt, instead of low-interest debt?

When you can't get a prime loan. So what does a prime loan mean? A prime loan has the lowest rates and the best terms available to borrowers.

You can qualify for a prime loan with a FICO score of 720 or better. I'll describe more about FICO scores in Chapter 8, but for now the important point is that when you don't have a prime loan, you get something punitive in the form of high-interest debt.

High Interest, Fees, and the Terrible Irony of Being Broke

Life is not fair, and high interest loans and fees are one of the unfairest parts of financial life. The less money you have, the more lenders will charge you. In that sense, lenders kick you when you're down. It's the truth.

When you have subprime or high-interest loans, the interest rate isn't the only thing you'll pay extra for. You'll also end up paying extra fees, penalties, origination fees, or "points" to get your high-interest loan, which makes borrowing even more expensive than the stated interest rate.

A well-known comic made this point a little while ago in a hilarious, awful, and true description of dealing with his bank when he was broke. I'll paraphrase his monologue:

Bank: "Uh sir, do you know you have insufficient funds in your checking account?"

Comic: "Yes, I'm aware, I don't have any money. But, that phrase 'insufficient funds,' yes, that's a nice way of putting it. I'm fucking broke."

Bank: "Well, we've had to charge you $25 because you only have $15 in your account and you attempted to—"

Comic: "Wait, you just took $25 from me, simply because I only had $15?"

Bank: "Yes, you see, sir, you had insufficient funds."

Comic: "Ok, yes, obviously as you say I don't have any money, but you took the little bit I did have, just because I don't have enough? And now that means I have less than zero dollars in my account. I have like, negative $10?"

Bank: "Yes, sir, because of your insufficient funds."

Comic: "But that means I can't even afford something that costs me zero money. Like, if somebody offered me something for free, I'd have to say, sorry, I don't even have zero dollars. Your free thing costs me zero dollars? That's too much. I can't even afford that much."

That's a tragicomic and accurate description of the way lenders treat people who don't have enough money. You pay extra, which seems like punishment for not having enough money in the first place. Which is awful. And true, because life is not fair, especially financial life.

You want more truth about the unfairness? Many lenders don't really want to "cure" your situation, because charging lots of extra "insufficient funds" fees as well as high interest on your debt can be quite lucrative for them.

For some lenders, charging those insufficient funds and late fees and high interest rates is the main business model for their profitability. In software programming terms, your bounced checks and late fees for them are a "feature" not a "bug" of their loan to you. They're charging you more money because you don't have enough money. With high-interest debt you are on a fast-moving treadmill designed to exhaust you, and you cannot win.

And even more truth: only you can cure your situation.

The cure is to pay off the debt, and to, over time, zealously guard your credit score so that you can qualify for low-interest debt.

Low-interest debt, as I'll explain in more detail in Chapter 8, doesn't prevent you from getting wealthy, and may actually be helpful to your wealth-building process.

Compounding Effect of High-Interest Debt

So how do I know there's such a big difference between high-interest debt and low-interest debt? Really, how do I know you cannot get wealthy if you carry high-interest debt, but you could get wealthy if you have some low-interest debt?

I know because I wield compound interest math like a ninja, and after reading Chapter 4 hopefully you do, too.

Let me introduce you to an elegant illustration called the Allowance Experiment that I learned from Andrew Tobias, author of the excellent *The Only Investment Guide You'll Ever Need*.[1]

Since you've mastered the lessons of Chapter 4 on compound interest (right?), you can follow right along with the math of the Allowance Experiment.

---

[1]Andrew Tobias, *The Only Investment Guide You'll Ever Need* (New York: Mariner Books, 2010), 225–228.

The Allowance Experiment

I actually did the allowance experiment with my eldest daughter. I presented her with two glass jars, each with one dollar already in it. I told her I agreed every day to add to the first jar an amount equal to 10% of whatever was in glass jar 1. I explained that in this way I would represent for her an optimistic view of how money wisely invested could grow over the long run.

(Just between you and me, 10% is probably too aggressive an annual return for ordinary investing over 35 years, but it has the virtue of being a nice round number. It is also not impossible as a long-term return. Including the reinvestment of dividends and price appreciation, the S&P 500 stock index compounded above 10% over the past 40 years.)

Because this ends up as a reasonable amount of money, I agree that this will be her allowance for the next 5 weeks.

I then tell her we will track how banks charge interest on credit cards, which can be 20% or more. To track that, each day I will add an amount equal to 20% of whatever is in glass jar 2.

The point here is to illustrate the difference that compounding interest makes—the difference between 10% and 20%—when you compound the effects over time. This is my way of teaching how the long-term effects of high interest are just too destructive for your wealth-building project.

I had her record in her journal the amount to add each day.

In jar 1, on day 1, that's a dime. Day 2, I put in 11 cents, because there's already $1.10 in the jar. Day 3, there's $1.21, so I add 12 cents. Each day I add 10% to the total, as her allowance, and I do that for 35 days.

You remember from Chapter 4 that I can figure out the total amount that will be in the jar using the formula $FV = PV * (1 + Y)^N$, where $PV = \$1$, $Y = 10\%$, and $N = 35$.

In jar 2, in the 20% high-interest jar that mimics credit card rates, we also start with one dollar.

I agree to put in 20% of the amount in the jar. So day 1 I add two dimes, because that's 20% of a dollar. Day 2, we've already got $1.20 in the jar, so 20% of that is 24 cents, which I drop in the jar. On day 3 the high-interest jar has $1.44, so I add in 29 cents. I also do this for 35 days.

Again, remembering the formula for compounding from Chapter 4, we can figure out the total amount that will be in the jar after 35 days using the formula $FV = PV * (1 + Y)^N$, where $PV = \$1$, $Y = 20\%$, and $N = 35$.

After 35 days the 10% allowance jar will have $28.10. Which is a lot, considering we started with a just a dollar and simply compounded at 10% per day. My daughter got to keep that, because I am a nice daddy.

After 35 days of compounding at 20%, however, the high-interest jar would have $590.67 in it.

Which is a whole other order of magnitude. The amount in the 20% interest rate is not around two times as much as the 10% jar, as you might casually and incorrectly guess without thinking too much about it.

It's 21 times as much money. My daughter did not get to keep that, because I am a nice daddy, but not that nice.

A credit card lender, which can certainly charge you 20% or more on your high-interest debt, and then continuously reinvest the payments it receives every year in other high-interest loans, could conceivably grow its original one dollar into $590.67 over 35 years.

Obviously, I've simplified the credit card business considerably to illustrate the long-term difference in interest rates.

Just as obvious, I hope, is the fact that when you agree to borrow money and pay high interest rates, you agree to make your lender rich and yourself poor.

Appendix

I'd like to qualify what I said in this chapter about utter simplicity—specifically the idea that you can forget everything else there is to know about personal finance, if you have high-interest debts and singularly focus on that problem.

If you have high-interest credit card debt, for example, should you only pay that down, or maybe should you do other things like contribute to your retirement accounts or buy a house?

Well, maybe. I'll allow for a bit of nuance.

From a pure finance standpoint—meaning taking into account just the numbers and mathematics of the case—focusing purely on paying down your high-interest debt usually makes the most sense.

What I mean by that is that if you carry a credit card balance on which you pay a 20% annual rate per month, the pure math suggests that you pay that down to zero before, say, contributing to an investment account, where you should not expect to beat a 20% return on investment. With this pure math perspective, it makes no sense to pay 20% on a $5,000 balance (paying $1,000 in interest per year), while earning say, an average 6% return on your $5,000 investment (earning $300 per year). You're $700 poorer at the end of the year, obviously.

Two factors make the decision a bit less clear than that, however.

One factor is psychology. The second factor is the possibility of a company match in a retirement account, and the tax advantages of retirement savings.

I'll take these one at a time.

Psychology

Psychologically speaking, your mountain of high-interest credit card debt may seem so high right now that you neglect to make other important wealth-building decisions. And if you delay certain decisions such as contributions to a retirement account indefinitely, then you may "never get there."

Again, the numbers don't necessarily support this thought—we're in the mushy realm of human psychology—but wealth building is not a purely numbers-based challenge. Maybe, possibly, small steps toward things like homeownership and retirement investments—even while still trying to address your high-interest credit card debt—can improve your chances of homeownership and having enough when you retire.

The Richest Man in Babylon Formula

One of the wisest books on personal finance—George Clason's *The Richest Man in Babylon*—posits a simple formula that may be helpful to you, if you have high-interest credit card debt.[2] Clason advocated living on 70% of your take-home pay, allocating 20% of your income to paying your debts, and then setting aside 10% to "pay yourself," meaning savings and eventually investments in retirement accounts, and saving to buy a home. The long-term effect of this is that even while you pay down your high-interest debts you are setting the foundation for long-term wealth building. By the time your debts get fully blasted away, you're well on your way to the next important goals for wealth. Like I said, I'm not convinced the pure math supports Clason's advice, but I do think the psychological effect may outweigh the numbers.

Even if the math isn't totally clear, parts of it are compelling, so I'll hum a few more bars on the math.

The Company Match

When it comes to contributing to a retirement account instead of paying off high-interest debt, a few factors work in favor of contributing to retirement accounts while allowing your mountain of high-interest debt to continue to exist a bit longer.

First, if you have access through your job to a 401(k) or 403(b) retirement account (more on these in Chapter 9!), some employers offer free employer matching funds for a portion of your retirement account contributions. As an employee making a contribution, this is nearly the only known instance in the universe of "free money" for you. Since free money from your employer is

---

[2]Some people swear by George Clason's 1926 classic book on indebtedness, savings, and compound interest, and certainly for memorable faux-babylonian parables and simple storytelling, it's a winner. George S. Clason, *The Richest Man in Babylon* (Reprint Edition by Dauphin Publications, 2015).

an instant, guaranteed, 100% return on your investment, it can make mathematical sense to contribute to an employer-matched retirement account instead of paying back even your high-interest credit card debt. How much should you contribute in this case? The clear math would suggest that you contribute at least as much to your retirement account as is necessary to take full advantage of an employer match.

(Parenthetically speaking, payday loans at above 100% annual interest rate are another, less-attractive story. Pay those down to zero first, no matter what.)

Tax Effects and Personal Net Worth

The tax advantages of retirement accounts also muddy the previously clear waters a bit. If you earn money in a 25% income tax bracket, for example, your contributions to a 401(k) or 403b or traditional IRA account provide an immediate 25% annual "return" on your money, since you don't pay taxes on any qualified amount you contribute to one of these retirement accounts.

Perhaps an example will help illustrate this.

Let's say you have $10,000 in high-interest credit card debt, charging you 25% per year in interest. That means you're obligated to pay $2,500 every year in interest just to carry that balance.

Now let's also say by happenstance you managed to get an extra $13,333.33 bonus this year. The choice you face is between paying off your high-interest credit card debt and/or funding a retirement account.

Choice 1: You take your bonus, subtract out the 25% federal income tax rate on your earned income, and you're left with exactly $10,000, just enough to pay off the high-interest debt entirely. That will save you $2,500 per year in interest charges, which would be awesome. You wouldn't have any money left over, but the boost to your future take-home pay from not making future credit card interest payments should help improve your lifestyle from here on out.

Choice 2: You could elect to contribute some of that bonus to your retirement account. To keep the math easy, for example, let's say you contribute $3,333.33 to a retirement account, leaving you with an after-tax take-home pay of $7,500, because the federal government claimed 25% of your post-contribution bonus of $10,000. Remember, after contributing to your retirement account, you end up paying taxes on only the extra $10,000 earned, not the full $13,333.33 bonus.

Now, $7,500 isn't enough to fully pay down your credit card debt, but it's a lot.

The after-tax result of choice 2 is that you'd take home $7,500 with which you pay down your debts, you'd pay $2,500 in federal income taxes, you'd still owe $2,500 on your credit card balance, and you'd now have an additional $3,333.33 in your retirement account. Because of the tax advantage of a retirement account, your net worth is $833.33 higher under this second scenario—making a retirement account contribution—than it would have been had you only paid off your high-interest debts with your bonus.

Your higher net worth comes at a cost, of course. You're still on the hook for an interest payment of $625 next year, because that's 25% of the remaining $2,500 high-interest credit card balance. While you cannot expect your $3,333.33 in retirement investment to generate the equivalent of a 25% return to keep pace with the high interest you owe next year, still the increase in net worth, plus the psychological effect of a greater net worth could make this an attractive—or at least plausibly responsible—use for your money, instead of simply paying down high-interest debt.

Furthermore and remember, if your $3,333.33 retirement account contribution in choice 2 qualified for employer matching funds, then the net worth advantage of choice 2 looks even better.

So like I said, simple still works when it comes to the overwhelming goal of paying down high-interest debt, but a little bit of nuance can be OK, too.

CHAPTER SEVEN

On Saving

On the financial monorail of life, we either work twice as hard as everyone else just to break even, or we glide easily ahead because our financial monorail gives us a helpful push forward.

In the former case, high-interest debt is the monorail against us. In the latter case, accumulated investments create wealth for us even while we're resting at our leisure. That's the whole point of Chapters 3, 4, 5, and 6 summarized in two sentences.

This chapter is about neither the forward nor the backward monorail. Rather, this chapter is about the one thing that allows you to hop off the backward-moving track and shifts you on to the forward-moving track: personal savings.

Now, for all of the tricks and tips written about saving money, saving money is not actually complicated. At the risk of sounding super-pedantic about it, we have to make sure that the amount of money coming into our account per month is larger than the amount of money going out of our account per month. Do this for a while and you will accumulate savings. Do this for a long time and you should end up wealthy.

This sounds kind of basic, I know.

"You can never be too rich or too thin," goes the old saying, and you might mistakenly think that the route to a svelte body or a fat wallet would involve hidden secrets and sophisticated techniques. Certainly, the Financial Infotainment Industrial Complex would have you believe in secrets and complicated techniques. Stay skeptical.

Nope. A svelte body is accomplished by the same basic method as savings. Make sure you have more calories expended per month than you take in during the month. Maintain this calorie deficit every month, and you will get thinner.

Similarly, with a money surplus every month, you will build savings. That is all.

But wait. That is not really all.

Since 90% of us don't feel we have a svelte enough body for our liking, nor enough accumulated savings for getting wealthy, my simple rule can't really be all.

The key to accumulating savings lies partially in the above basic truth and maybe more importantly in the complicated realm of human psychology.

In the second part of this chapter I'll review some of the specific techniques that could work for you if you are beginning to save, or if you want to increase your savings. What works for you, however, depends mostly on your own mind, because the biggest barrier to savings is in our mind.

I know, I know, that sounds crazy. Because you might be under the impression that the biggest barrier to savings is that you don't make enough money. Fine, you have a point. You don't make enough. I agree.

But allow me to let you in on a little secret about saving money: nobody feels like they earn enough to save money. I really mean nobody.

Now, that's an odd thing to say, because you've no doubt read about public figures who earn extraordinary paychecks.

Take, for example, 13-year NFL veteran star Warren Sapp, who earned millions of dollars as a successful football player, and then transitioned to a television commentator and *Dancing with the Stars* contestant earning over a million dollars per year after his playing career ended. Or perhaps you remember boxing champion Mike Tyson, who earned $300 million from his fights. Or popular music stars like Billy Joel, Natalie Cole, or Michael Jackson. Surely they made enough money?

All of those big-time earners named in the paragraph above declared bankruptcy or were wiped out by tens of millions of dollars in debt, despite tens, to hundreds, of millions in earnings.

For them, there was no amount of money sufficient to cover the costs of their lifestyle. The problem was never their thin paycheck, but rather their fat expenses.

On the other end of the earnings spectrum, somehow people manage to save money while earning comparatively little. What I mean is, if you make $50,000 per year, you probably live near someone who makes 20% less than you, say, $40,000 a year.

Now, you have no money left over at the end of the month at $50,000 per year. I know.

It sucks. Somehow, however, your neighbor making $40,000 has figured out how to pay all of her bills. She even socks away an extra few hundred dollars every month! How does she do it?

I don't know how your neighbor does it. I mean, I have a few guesses. I'll share them later in this chapter. Oddly enough, however, your neighbor earning $40,000 also knows somebody getting by on just $32,000 a year, and can't figure out how that's done. Meanwhile, in another part of town, a family of four is unable to save any money on $160,000 per year. Their debts just pile up. It's weird. This is the point: it's not really about the amount of money you earn.

The margin for error is obviously much smaller for the $40,000 earner. Many more people can build up savings making $160,000 per year, but also many can't. As incredible as it sounds to someone making $40,000 per year, it's quite easy to have zero savings on a $160,000 salary per year.

The point is to notice the mystery of savings has less to do with raw earning power and more to do with personal behaviors and lifestyle costs. It has to do with what and how you spend. Just like the key to weight control is limiting calorie intake, the key to savings is limiting money outflow.

Now, I know this is all very theoretical and maybe you'd like to get a bit more practical. Like, how do you actually save money?

The Role of Budgeting: Hawthorne Effect

At this point in the savings narrative, many would-be financial advice-givers start to get very pushy about the importance of budgeting. Not being a budgeter myself, I feel unprepared to advocate it for others. Personally, I don't find budgeting a sustainable activity in my life. Maybe you do. Or maybe you will. That's fine. I'm not going to get pushy about it.

However, if you do have trouble limiting your lifestyle costs, I do think budgeting at least for some period of time can create a positive psychological effect, by what's known as the Hawthorne or observer effect. Scientific researchers have long known that observing phenomenon can change the thing you observe. The very act of observing something, such as keeping track of your budget, can change your behavior. Specifically, if you start tracking every expenditure—including Tic-Tacs in the checkout line and $0.99 iTunes downloads—you probably will reduce your actual purchases. It's a small trick, but it might be a way to make budgeting useful to you. The Hawthorne effect is kind of the main point of budgeting, in my opinion.

Although that's not the entire story.

The Latte Effect

I once did a little experiment in budgeting, for just 1 week, which you might want to try yourself.

I decided to track—through an iPhone app—the amount I spent per week just on premium coffee. If you've got a similar addictive vice like mine to caffeine, maybe you'd like to attempt a little budgeting experiment like this. I knew I frequently spent money on coffee, but I hadn't bothered to add up all of my teensy tiny little expenditures.

I was stunned to learn at the end of the week that I'd spent $40.14 at the coffee shop. Some of that was the coffee, some of that was the extra unnecessary muffin to accompany the coffee, and once it was the lunch I grabbed because I happened to be in a coffee shop.

I'm wholly convinced that we all have these little unnecessary expenditures. Your thing might not be coffee, but it's probably something. Only you know what that something is. Try tracking it for a week or month to see the cumulative effect of your little "nothing" expenditure.

Now, $40.14 in a week seemed like much more than I expected. But at the same time, was it large enough to matter in the grand scheme of things? The amount of $40.14 per week isn't the difference between being rich and poor, is it?

Spoiler alert: it is.

The personal finance author David Bach, who coined the term "latte effect" to describe my (as well as your) unnecessary $40.14 addiction, urges us to become aware of our own latte effects, whatever they may be.

Chapter 4 on compound interest gave us the tools to figure out the difference that $40.14 can make on a life of savings and investments. So let's do some very quick math using compound interest. I know from the 1-week budgeting exercise that my "latte effect" is $40.14 per week, which adds up to $2,087.28 after 52 weeks.

What if, instead of satisfying my caffeine addiction, I saved the latte money one year and invested it in a mutual fund that tracked the stock market. If I did this single prudent thing at age 25 and managed to earn a 6% return every year until I turned 75 years old, I'd be how much richer?

Recall that compound interest can be calculated as $FV = PV * (1+Y)^N$, where the PV is $2,087.28, the Y is 6%, and the N is 50.

So the future value of 1 year's latte effect savings, 50 years later, is $38,448.02. That's pretty good, although I'm not sure it's life changing in retirement.

If I earned 10% in the stock market, 50 years later I'd be $245,027.58 richer. Now we're closer to life altering. You should plug those numbers into your spreadsheet and verify the compound interest math. I'll be right here until you get back.

OK, welcome back.

Now maybe you don't think a 10% annual return is reasonable. You might be right. Although just so you know, the broad stock market represented by the S&P 500, including reinvestment of dividends, has earned more than that per year over the course of my lifetime. So, a 10% return is admittedly optimistic, but also realistic, based on my own observable experience.

And that's all just from one single year of savings and investment discipline. But what if I had never become addicted to caffeine in the first place?

What if I managed to save and invest my latte affect amount every year between age 25 and 75?

To answer that question I'd create a spreadsheet list of 50 years' worth of compound interest calculations. The first year, earning 6% on the original $2,087.28 for 50 years, becomes $38,448.02. The second year, earning 6% for 49 years, becomes $36,271.72. The third year, earning 6% for 48 years, becomes $34,218.60, and so on for the next 50 years.

At the end, by age 75, my spreadsheet tells me my net worth is higher by $642,373.07. All from cutting out a tiny amount of savings—a single vice!—from my daily habits, and investing it.

If I run the same compound interest math but use a 10% return, my latte effect over 50 years nets me $2,672,343.29. Now, who wants to be a millionaire?

What Is the Real Point?

You might misinterpret this whole exercise as an anti-caffeine screed. Nothing could be further from the truth. You could no more successfully separate me from my coffee than you could pry a baby kangaroo from its mother's pouch. Don't even try it with me.

I'm not saying you should never spend money on things that give you joy. As coffee does for me.

What I'm really saying is that very small changes in weekly and monthly savings, dedicated to a good investment plan (for that, see Chapters 13 and 14) over the long run, make an extraordinary difference in terms of net worth. The amount of $40.14 per week is nothing. Really. It's just $5.73 per day. Do you have that amount you could save per day?

The point of doing a budget, for me, is to figure out if you are spending $5.73 per day more than you need to. Or maybe $3 more than you need to. Or maybe $73 per day more than you need to. I don't know which one is more true for you. I mean, I'm pretty sure it's something.

So while I don't think you should have to cut out caffeine (or your own vice of choice) necessarily, nor do I think you should budget for your whole life, I do think budgeting, as a way to identify where and how a few dollars a day of savings could be found, could be the key to savings. It could be the key to becoming a millionaire over your lifetime.

Automation

Having gotten this far into the savings discussion, I have yet to mention the single most important technique for actually building up savings. We haven't yet described the best way in which you should take your $3, or $5.73, or $73 per day and actually save it. Now, it is time. Are you ready?

Automation.

I only know of one nearly foolproof way to save money, and that's to automate the savings. What I mean by that is to create a "set it and forget it" rule with your bank account. A rule something along the lines of "every paycheck I whisk away $x into a saving account that I can't easily access." Or, every day, I move $3 from my checking account into a savings account, ideally a savings account that I can't get to very well.

Automatic deductions force us to do something nobody wants to do, which is forgo spending all of our money today for the benefit of some uncertain tomorrow.

Admittedly, automatic deductions are not strictly "rational." Why should it matter if money sits in one checking account or sits in a separate savings account? Nothing has changed except where the money sits. And yet, everything is changed. For some reason, if we can remove money from our typical "spending account," we can avoid spending it.

Technology allows us to accomplish this mind trick more easily than ever. Your bank very likely allows you to set up a rule for moving money on a regular, automated basis. It doesn't matter which rule you set, but you should try some "set it and forget it" rule. Try every week, or every paycheck, or every month. Just try something in an automated way. It works.

A funny mobile app named Qapital takes the same principle of savings through automation and extends it into clever paths. You can move a set amount of money from your checking account into a savings account whenever your favorite (or least favorite) politician tweets. You can automate the movement of money whenever you hit, or don't hit, a certain fitness target. You can move the "roundups" or spare change from your debit card purchases, on a weekly basis. Or when you shop at a store. Or buy your latte. Qapital is just the latest way to build on the true insight that automation is the best way to accumulate savings, to "set it and forget it."

Automated savings always start out small and seem like they might not lead to much over time. I'd urge you to remain optimistic, however, and remember the compound interest effects of small amounts of money. That optimism will make your fortune.

While automation works better than anything else I know, a few other high-value techniques might work to help you save money as well.

Paying Cash

Some people swear by this, including two variations on the original theme I'll describe below. In its simplest form, paying cash forces you to only spend what you literally have at present, rather than charging purchases on a high-interest credit card that will be paid in the future. If limiting your purchases to cash helps you avoid credit card fees and interest, I'm all for it.

Some people take out a set amount of cash from the bank at the beginning of a month, and then try to survive by only spending their physical cash. At the checkout counter, with just $12 in hand, they can't impulse purchase above the $12 limit. If that helps as a reminder that money is finite, that's fine by me, too.

A variation on this all-cash theme that some people swear by is the "envelope trick." With this, you label physical envelopes things like "Grocery Money," and "Entertainment," and "School Supplies," and withdraw a set amount of cash from the bank to fill the envelope at the beginning of the month, or at the beginning of a pay cycle. If the money in the envelope runs out, you just have to do without that category of expenses, until the next pay cycle.

Because most large expenditures are due monthly, like car payments, housing payments, personal loans, insurance, and utilities, I think creating envelope budgets only makes sense on a monthly basis.

I've experimented with the envelope trick in my family and have admittedly never gotten it to work properly. But hey, it might be just the thing you need to kick-start your savings program. Like I said, some people swear by it.

Bargaining with Cash Only

Another variation on the cash-only theme is the idea of withdrawing a set cash amount in advance of a large purchase, like furniture, or a used car. Employed correctly, this technique absolutely works for saving money.

You've spotted a couch you need to buy at the store. Or you have a good lead on a car at the dealership. Or a washer-dryer set at the appliance store. Setting a top-limit budgeted amount ahead of time, and holding that precise amount of cash in your hands, gives you an unusual bargaining position with the person selling. Whatever the listed price, you can try offering less money, in the amount that fits your budget. Most brick-and-mortar stores that sell higher-price items, like cars and furniture and appliances, expect and allow some negotiation on prices like this, even if they do not advertise it.

If your $600 offer for an $800 item gets turned down initially, you might just want to remove the cash from your pocket. "I'm sorry," you might say, waving the bills, "but I only have this amount of money saved up for this purchase. I can give you this $600 and you can make the sale today. If not, I have to walk out today and end up buying from someone else."

This does not work every time, of course. It won't work either with the increasing amount of shopping we all do online. But it will work more often than you expect with in-person purchases at brick-and-mortar stores. You may feel squeamish, initially, about this hard-nosed technique. You may decide, however, that $200 in savings is worth 10 minutes of squeamishness. I mean, would you spend 10 minutes on your hands and knees uncomfortably trying to fish out $200 in bills wedged into the tiny space underneath the front seat of your car? I know I would. Think of earning that $200 through a little temporary discomfort. I mean, $200 for 10 minutes is a pretty good rate.

Also, never forget that the salesperson who accepts your offer for $600, sighing heavily all the way, secretly is thrilled to have made the sale. Otherwise your offer would not have been accepted. Paying with just the limited amount of cash literally in your hand at the store is what makes your offer credible, and effective.

Finally, paying cash encourages a more modest purchase. If you limit yourself to $600 in cash for the furniture set, you have just saved yourself from the $2,400 splurge on a fancier, flashier furniture option that was available only with high-interest credit. Modesty, as always, aligns well with wealth building.

Emergency Fund

Finally, a few words about the classic personal finance trope on saving money: "First," the advice goes, "build an emergency fund."

Count me as deeply skeptical of that advice.

In my experience, people who need an emergency fund rarely build one. Of course, it would be nice to have a little extra money in a savings account. Because having money is generally better than not having it.

But realistically, people who are given the advice "build an emergency fund" typically suffer from high-interest debt, like credit card loans. Paying down a credit card balance, typically charging 12% or 18% or 25%, is a far better idea than building up an emergency fund. If you have high-interest credit card debt at present, then you shouldn't have an emergency fund. You should work on getting your credit card balance to zero first. That zero-balance credit card with an unused available line for borrowing actually is your initial emergency fund.

On the other side, people who have zero balances on their credit card, or who are pretty good about saving money, don't really need one. Emergency funds are inefficient. They hardly earn any interest, generally, since they can't be invested in any risky way that earns a meaningful return.

You don't really need an emergency fund. What you need is "emergency liquidity." Meaning, if you can borrow the money in an emergency and pay it back within a reasonable amount of time—with a 3-week credit card loan, or with a HELOC[1] for a longer period of time—then an emergency fund is not only irrelevant but also expensive.

---

[1] I define HELOC in the next chapter, on low-interest debt.

The need for "emergency liquidity," not an "emergency fund," partly illustrates the value of low-interest debt—the topic of the next chapter.

For Further Reading

Among the simplest and most powerful books arguing for the application of the power of compound interest, plus the power of automated savings, is by David Bach, *The Automatic Millionaire: A Powerful One-Step Plan to Live and Finish Rich* (New York: Broadway Books, 2004).

A great description of the weird fact that nobody makes enough money to save, but somehow somebody else down the street earning less money than you is able to do it, can be found in the book by Andrew Tobias, *The Only Investment Guide You'll Ever Need* (New York: Mariner Books, 2010). Tobias also has a great section on tips for saving money.

CHAPTER EIGHT

On Low-Interest Debt

The great dividing line between sustainable and unsustainable debt is whether you must borrow at a high rate of interest or a low "prime" rate of interest. This is the difference between misery and happiness. Over a lifetime, it is the difference between wealth and no wealth.

A prime rate means the lowest available interest rate for a car loan, home loan, personal loan, student loan, or small-business loan. Banks and lenders offer the low-interest prime rate if they believe you are a low-risk prospect to borrow their money, which depends largely—although not exclusively—on your past borrowing record, as captured by your FICO score.

Recall from Chapter 3's monorail analogies: any time you borrow money you end up having to work extra hard just to remain in one place, due to the power of compound interest. This is true to an extent. As discussed in Chapter 6, carrying high-interest debt like credit cards, payday loans, subprime car loans, or subprime home loans is like running against a fast-moving monorail just to keep from falling behind. With high-interest debt, you will never get ahead and you will exhaust yourself. On the optimistic front, your financial path remains extraordinarily simple if you do one thing first: pay down that debt!

On the other hand, borrowing at a prime, or low, rate of interest makes for a slower monorail against you. Yes, you still have to walk fast or jog to keep up, but the burden isn't impossible. The point of this chapter is to give you permission to borrow money, as long as you borrow at the best terms. Used in moderation, low-interest debt can be compatible with, and even helpful for, building wealth.

As I already mentioned in Chapter 6, a certain type of finance guru popular these days advocates never borrowing money under any circumstances. I'm skeptical. The argument there is that the interest you pay will inevitably

Your FICO Score

What is a FICO score? Why is it important? Should you pay attention to it? When can you ignore it?

Borrowing at a low rate of interest for a car, house, or student loans depends in part on whether you have a high enough FICO score to qualify for a "prime" loan.

You can be a prime borrower if your FICO score remains above approximately 720 at one of the three credit bureaus—Equifax, Experian, or TransUnion. You will borrow at subprime (meaning, high) rates with a FICO of 650 or below. In between 650 and 720 in the mortgage banking world is called "Alt-A" and will not generally qualify you for the best rates with lenders.

The FICO score, created by the Fair Isaac Company, is a single number encapsulating your borrowing history. It's the equivalent of an SAT score for applications to college. FICO serves as a kind of sorting mechanism for lenders to know what kind of terms to offer you. A high FICO gets you the best interest rate available from most lenders. A low FICO gets you a higher interest rate, worse borrowing terms, or possibly no loan at all.

Your FICO score specifically derives from five factors:

1. The frequency of delinquent payments on your debts, as well as how recent those delinquencies are. Delinquencies lower your FICO.

2. The amount of debt you have now, including and especially compared to how much unused borrowing capacity you have. Less debt raises your FICO, and more borrowing capacity raises your FICO.

3. The length of time you have been a borrower. Longer raises your FICO, shorter lowers it.

4. Whether you have applied for credit recently, or have relatively new credit. New borrowing or new borrowing inquiries indicates your need for debt, which lowers your score.

5. The type of debt you have. Certain types of installment loans are considered riskier than mortgage debt, for example, and can lower your score.

Interestingly, your FICO score indicates nothing about your income, wealth, or employment status, although lenders care tremendously about all of these things as well. Your FICO also indicates nothing about demographic factors like race, religion, gender, marital status, and geography, and in that sense is a "fair" or "objective" measure based solely on your past and present experience with debt.

> The best way to repair your FICO score, if it's low, is to always pay all your debts on time. Timely payments, over time, will increase your score. Up until you obtain at least a 720, you will benefit as a borrower by improving your score. Lower interest rates save you money.
>
> Above 720, or maybe 750 at a stretch, you generally will not gain additional benefits as a prime borrower. Once you are able to get a low-interest prime loan the terms don't get any better.
>
> In an ideal world, you might ignore your FICO because you could pay cash for everything. Almost nobody lives in this ideal world. As a result, I strongly believe you should pay a little bit of money—around $15—to purchase your FICO score from one of the credit bureaus before you apply for a new loan. The knowledge of how a lender will evaluate you—prime, subprime, or Alt-A—will make you a smarter borrower.
>
> If you know you are currently considered subprime or Alt-A but have made steps that could improve your score in the coming months, it makes sense to wait until you hit prime status before taking out a big loan like a mortgage.

make you poorer—the monorail moving against you will prove too strong to overcome. And of course, "debt free" has a certain attraction in its uncompromising simplicity, like a hardcore prohibition on alcohol or caffeine consumption.

His case is medium strong when it comes to high interest, but less so for low-interest debt.

I'll explain why I believe this. Student loans and home mortgage loans—the two largest ways most of us will borrow money—justifiably constitute the two biggest investments you can make for creating wealth.

Borrowing money to educate yourself, either for a college degree or an advanced degree, means investing in your own human potential, something that enhances your earnings capacity. It may well enhance your soul. In that sense, there can be no greater investment. Borrowing money to purchase a home—as we shall see in Chapter 12—might be the biggest step you ever make to create wealth.

Borrowing at a low interest rate to purchase an affordable car, similarly, makes sense under most scenarios. As much as a car-free lifestyle might appeal to our aesthetic or moral outlook, the plain fact is that a car might be a key to getting or remaining employed.

At the risk of stating the obvious, you might need to borrow money to get the car in order to earn money, and if you can borrow at a low interest rate, these are all perfectly compatible choices with growing your wealth over the long run.

I'm mostly running through this easy thought process to point out that the hard-core debt-free financial gurus are overly strict in their pronouncements. For most of us, some low-interest debt is not only necessary, but wealth enhancing and, possibly, soul enhancing.

Yes, we can make errors when we borrow for education or borrow to buy a house, but the opportunity to enhance our life and wealth prospects, made

---

HELOC: Low-Interest Ninja-Style Debt

Quick warning: This description is mostly just for black-belt level financial ninjas, as an example of potentially dangerous, but also potentially wealth enhancing, low-interest debt. Don't try this if you have a previous problem paying off your debts.

HELOC stands for Home Equity Line of Credit, and I want to briefly mention HELOCs in the context of praising, or at least condoning, low-interest debt. In my own life, HELOCs have proved awesome.

If you own your home (see Chapter 12) and you owe on your mortgage less than 80% of the value of your home, you can usually get an additional line of credit based on the value of your home. This line of credit, known as the HELOC, can and should remain with a zero balance most of the time. An unused line of credit allows you to pay for things even if you don't have the money in the bank right now. But remember to leave it unused until you really need it.

This is absolutely a key point. If you have a $40,000 line of credit, for example, the idea here is that you don't draw on it unless something extremely important happens. That important thing could be the opportunity of a lifetime to purchase the empty lot next to your house. It could be for emergency medicals bills that hopefully only happen once in your life. The point is, don't use it for frivolous things. Frivolous use of the HELOC is madness and you could lose your house if everything went badly. Remain modest in your uses.

So why are they good then? First, HELOCs can be good because they provide immediate ready liquidity, which can work as a better substitute for the inefficient "emergency fund" I mentioned in Chapter 7.

Second, as a prime borrower with a HELOC, you can obtain very low interest rates, since the bank lends against the value of your home.

The ability to write a large check immediately on your HELOC, on short notice, arms you to opportunistically respond to financial opportunities or financial dangers. Ninja-style.

possible through debt, can't be denied. When we borrow at a low interest rate, the speed of the monorail working against us is slow enough that we can still make forward progress on building wealth. We can still do all the right things financially while working with low-interest debt.

The key is that borrowing at a *low rate of interest* makes the choice to borrow so much more likely to be compatible with building wealth.

Because we can carry low-interest debt and build wealth simultaneously, it isn't necessary to pay off every single low-interest debt we have before turning to other worthy uses of our money, such as opening a retirement account (Chapter 9) purchasing a home (Chapter 12), investing (Chapters 13 and 14), purchasing insurance (Chapter 16), estate planning (Chapter 19), starting our own business (Chapter 21), or giving money away (Chapter 21). Optimistically speaking, we'll move gradually toward debt-free living over the medium-term, while tackling these other wealth-building tasks sooner, rather than later.

Psychological vs. Mathematical Justification

If you've rid yourself of high-interest debt and only have prime-rate student loans, car loans, or mortgage loans, then the choice to tackle another wealth-enhancing task, instead of retiring debt, may come down to psychological preference rather than pure mathematics.

I mean, how much do you like being debt-free? Do you feel better with $5,000 in retirement savings and $10,000 in low-interest student loan debt, or do you feel better with $5,000 in low-interest student loans and zero in retirement savings? Mathematically, your personal financial "net worth" is the same either way. The difference in long-term wealth prospects between the two paths is not clearly distinguishable. Yes, it's always better to have less debt rather than more debt, but it's also better to start a retirement account early rather than late. Reasonable people can disagree.

I think the "right" answer in this case depends as much on your personal preference as on math. I don't know for certain which path is better specifically for you. I do know for certain that some low-interest debt is fine, especially if it was incurred for a good project, like education, a home, or an essential vehicle.

What about borrowing for other things? Borrowing for a vacation or your wedding or to buy a personal robot may be a top priority for you, but you won't get a blessing to borrow for that from me. For those other things, I'm going to lean closer to the hard-core debt-free position. Please note that low-interest borrowing for reasons beyond higher education, a home, or a car is typically less justifiable, from a personal finance perspective.

Can this "permission" to take out low-interest debt even for good things be abused? Of course. Remember, all debt is a prescription drug. Great for many, terrible for some. Plenty of education spending gets wasted. We can buy too much house with too much debt. There's a big difference between using debt to buy an unaffordable car versus buying an affordable car. Just because you can borrow does not mean you should borrow. Remaining modest in your debt-fueled consumption of even education, house, and car will greatly enhance your path to wealth.

CHAPTER NINE

On Retirement Accounts

Let's say you're 23. You have student loans. You don't make much money. Paying rent is a struggle. Maybe keeping up with monthly credit card debt payments consumes your financial brain. Why should you worry about retirement accounts now, when there's so much time to worry about that later, and also you don't have any extra money to fund your retirement?

To be clear, I understand retirement doesn't seem like it *should* be a top priority, nor does it seem like it *could* be a top priority.

But as Yogi Berra said, "it gets late early out there." Many a 50-year-old wakes up, absorbs the lessons of this chapter a few decades late, and regrets her earlier decades. The nature of investing and compound interest is this: small simple steps, taken early, turn out better than heroic actions taken late.

I'm here to say, optimistically, that once you've managed to wrestle high-interest debt down into no debt—or at least into low-interest debt—retirement accounts need to become your top financial priority. Even if you struggle with paying off high-interest credit card debt every month, it can make sense to fund retirement accounts, at least to a certain amount. Retirement accounts are not the tail end of personal financial planning and investing, but rather the beginning.

Ideally, you have a chance to start a retirement account through your job, such as a 401(k) or 403(b) account. Even without that option, you can always begin retirement savings with an individual retirement arrangement (IRA), if you have any income this year.

This chapter will define and describe the different retirement accounts currently available in the United States and the ways to prioritize them. Common questions you might struggle with include:

- Which account should you contribute to first?
- Traditional vs. Roth IRAs?

- Should you contribute to retirement accounts even if you have debt?
- Is it really necessary to start retirement investing early?
- Does it ever make sense to withdraw funds early?

We'll get to all that in this chapter, but let's first talk about the common features of tax-advantaged retirement accounts. There's no quiz later on this. You don't have to remember it all. I'm just laying these out there so we have some common knowledge base on which we can build in a few key points about retirement accounts.

The following features apply to all retirement accounts.

1. The original point of retirement accounts, as created by the U.S. Congress, is to give an income tax break to people earning income. This is meant to incentivize—via the tax break—long-term retirement savings by individuals.

2. The second point of retirement accounts is to offer tax-efficient investing over the long run. As a result, buying and selling stuff within your account—without making withdrawals—will save you from incurring "capital gains" taxes. Investment income in the form of dividends or interest—if not withdrawn from the account—are also not taxed. So we can potentially save both income taxes and capital gains taxes within our retirement accounts.

3. Despite, or because of, these tax breaks, the U.S. Congress doesn't want to make retirement accounts *too* generous. So there are limits to how much money any individual can contribute in any given year and still qualify for the tax incentive. Generally speaking, workplace accounts like 401(k) and 403(b) have higher contribution limits than nonworkplace accounts like an IRA.

4. Because people often have undercontributed to their retirement as they approach retirement age, these contribution limits are usually a bit higher after age 50.

5. In order to receive an income tax advantage on your contribution, you need to have at least earned as much in income in a year as you contribute to your account. So, if you only earn $4,000 this year, you may only make a maximum contribution of $4,000 this year.

6. You have until the income tax filing deadline, usually on or around April 15, to make a tax-advantaged contribution to a retirement account for the previous year. So you generally have an extra 3.5 months after the end of the calendar year to max out your contributions.

7. If you've given the maximum allowable amount for last year during that 3.5-month time window, for example, you may still contribute the maximum allowable amount to the same account for the next year.

8. Contributing money to a retirement account, preferably held at a brokerage firm, allows you to invest in a wide menu of investment products, typically

stocks or bonds or mutual funds. Banks and insurance companies, in addition to brokerage firms, also offer retirement accounts, although I find their typical investment menus less appropriate for retirement accounts. You are even allowed to also invest in other more exotic investment products, such as real estate or commodities or private funds or private businesses, although you would need specialized retirement sponsors for that approach, and more specialized advice to avoid running afoul of IRS restrictions on retirement account investing. For the purposes of this book, which is all about simplicity, I'm going to ignore those more specialized opportunities.

9. Some people confuse the following point, so it deserves emphasis. The specific investments inside a retirement account will determine your long-run results. These results can be terrible, middling, or excellent, depending on the specific investments chosen. The fact that money or an investment sits inside your IRA or 401(k) does not guarantee a specific return or amount of risk. You choose the specific investment and risk yourself, and that makes all the difference in the long run.

10. Taking money out of your retirement account before an official retirement age, currently 59.5, can incur a penalty such as 10%, plus income taxes owed on the withdrawn amount. Certain exceptions for hardship may let you skip the penalty, although not the taxes.

11. Because the U.S. Congress wants to eventually tax your money, you must start withdrawing from your retirement accounts by a certain age, currently 70.5. Each year after that, the IRS mandates that a percentage of your account be withdrawn—and taxed—according to a schedule that takes into account your expected years of life remaining. This amount that you withdraw in your retirement years, called the required minimum distribution (RMD), allows the IRS to tax withdrawals as income. The general rule I've described here does not apply to so-called Roth retirement accounts, because contributions, not withdrawals, were already taxed.

OK, phew, that's a lot of rules. No need to memorize them. Like I said, there will be no quiz. I just wanted to list them all for your future reference. All of that will make it easier to discuss the specific features of existing retirement plans.

The U.S. Congress periodically creates (or discontinues) the retirement accounts available to savers, so this specific information may change over time. The U.S. Congress also periodically updates the contribution limits for 401(k) and IRA accounts, so the numbers described in this chapter will likely increase over time. Despite these changes, the principles—start early, get matching funds, automate contributions, and maximize contributions if you can—likely will not change.

So here are the different accounts you could know about. Again, I've listed a bunch of semitechnical information below, not in the hopes that you'll absorb it all on the first read-through, but rather because maybe you'll bookmark this section. When you need to know it, you can come back to the paragraph that tells you what you need to know.

Individual Retirement Arrangement (IRA)

An IRA is an account to which anyone below retirement age, with income, may contribute. The traditional IRA offers an income tax deduction in the year of the contribution. Contributors to a Roth IRA do not receive an income tax deduction. Individuals will typically open up an IRA with a brokerage company (preferred), an insurance company, or a bank, each of which will offer a menu of investment options. When funds are withdrawn from a Roth in retirement, however, withdrawals may be taken tax-free. If you make a relatively high income, you may become ineligible for the tax deduction at the time of contribution, and you may also become ineligible to contribute to a Roth IRA. The contribution limit at the time of this writing is $5,500, or $6,500 for contributors over age 50.

401(k)

A 401(k) is an employer-sponsored retirement plan, for employees of for-profit companies. The sponsor of the plan, chosen by the employer, offers a menu of investment options. At the end of employment with that company, employees may roll over their 401(k) plans into what's called a "rollover IRA," without having to withdraw funds, lose their tax-advantaged status, or pay taxes or penalties. Some employers allow departed employees to leave funds where they are even after leaving employment, although some don't.

One of the most attractive parts of a 401(k) plan is that employers sometimes make matching contributions to incentivize employees to save for retirement. More on that below. Contribution limits are generally higher than an IRA, and as of this writing are $18,500. For employer-sponsored plans like a 401(k), companies may elect to contribute "profit-sharing" payments to employees, which can significantly raise the annual contribution into a retirement account, beyond the employee's $18,500 limit. Some employers allow employees to make contributions to a Roth 401(k), forgoing an income tax break in the year of the contribution, but enjoying tax-free income in retirement from withdrawals.

403(b): This closely resembles the features of a 401(k) plan, but are offered to nonprofit employees and public employees. Contribution limits are the same as a 401(k).

457: This tax-advantaged account is offered to highly compensated nonprofit and public employees who may receive deferred compensation, aka compensation usually paid after retirement. Employees who qualify can typically contribute to both a 457 account and a 403(b) account.

SIMPLE IRA: An employer-sponsored account considered lower cost and lower complexity for employers to administer, as compared to a 401(k) plan. These have a mandatory employer match. Contribution limits are lower than a 401(k) and are $12,500 as of this writing.

SEP: A retirement plan for self-employed businesspeople. As of this writing, these had a $54,000 maximum annual contribution limit.

Individual 401(k): Like a SEP, this plan allows individual business owners to have a 401(k) plan, and the maximum individual contribution as of this writing was $54,000.

Matching Employer Funds: The Only Free Lunch You'll Ever Find in Finance

As much as I won't blame you for semi-skipping over the preceding menu of retirement accounts and their features, now is the time to sit up straight and pay attention. Because: free money.

Every economist will tell you "there's no free lunch." Economists also tell the joke that if you find a $100 bill on the sidewalk, it could not possibly exist, since in a rational world it would have been picked up by now. And yet, economists will also join me in advocating you take advantage of the "free lunch" offered by employer matching funds in a 401(k) or 403(b) account.

Employers frequently, but not always, offer to match employee contributions to 401(k) or 403(b) accounts. That match might be the first $1,000 you contribute per year, for example, or the first $7,000, or the first 3% of your salary. In any case, in any amount, this is "free money" for you as an employee.

Can I have your attention, please? These employer-matched funds make contributing to your 401(k)-style retirement account the single most obviously good personal finance move out there. I know of no other "free lunch" on the planet.

If you have very little money every month and are trying to choose between competing needs, I'm here to tell you that the most important need is to contribute to your 401(k) *at least up to the amount matched by your employer.* You have to take the free lunch. Of course you should aspire to make the maximum contribution each year to your 401(k), because of the tax advantages, automation, and long-term prospects for growing your wealth. If you must contribute less than the maximum, however, please don't lose out on the free lunch. Do this even before fully paying off your credit card, as crazy as that sounds. Your credit card may charge you 20% per year, but the return on your employer match is an immediate 100%.

High Interest Debt vs. Retirement Account Investing

That brings up an important question—one posed in fact in the title to this book. Should you make contributions to your retirement accounts, even if you have debt?

The answer—OK, now I sound like one of those annoying wishy-washy economists I referenced in the last section—is that *it depends*. But probably, yes, you should.

I'll explain. If you only have low-interest-rate debt as described in Chapter 8—such as student loans, a prime mortgage, a prime car loan, or a home equity line of credit—then for sure you should be turning your attention to filling up your retirement account. By investing for the long run in your retirement account, you will very likely earn more than you currently pay on that low-interest debt. You might pay 5% on your low-interest debt, for example, and in the long run should be able to beat that rate with your investments, if done properly (see Chapters 13, 14, and 15).

If you have high-interest debt, then the answer becomes a bit trickier, but in many cases is still yes. If you pay interest on credit cards charging you a 20% interest rate, a logical finance and mathematics thought is that you can't beat 20% per year with your investments. I know that's true, or at least it's true in the long run. (In the short run, obviously, anything is possible.)

Since you probably pay a 25% or 30% income tax rate, however, the pure math calculation changes. In the year of your contribution to your retirement account, you've automatically "earned" the marginal tax rate on your contribution. What I mean by that obtuse finance-speak is that a $4,000 contribution to your retirement account will "save" you from having to pay $1,000 in taxes, if you have a 25% income tax rate. That's why it can make some sense to make a tax-deductible IRA contribution even if you pay 20% on your credit card.

I know, I know, this is all a bit theoretical, since if you don't have money to pay for your credit card debt you probably also won't have money for your retirement account. But still, a case can be made for even the mathematical logic of a retirement account contribution, even with high-interest debt.

The long run answer of course remains (as mentioned in Chapter 6) that it's difficult to impossible to consistently engage in wealth building if you pay high interest on your debts, like credit card debt.

Automation

As I mentioned in Chapter 7 on savings, the true secret to making retirement contributions is automation. Workplace accounts like a 401(k) or 403(b) make automated contributions easy, since you will have funds regularly withdrawn from your paycheck automatically, before your greedy little hands get the money. Savings, retirement contributions, and investments that seem impossible suddenly become possible when we create an automated process month after month, year after year.

If you can manage to automate and maximize your retirement contributions—through a "set it and forget it" process—you should end up wealthy in the long run. Trust me.

To fully take advantage of the magic of automation, you should also look into automating your IRA contributions from your bank account. This is probably a few minutes' worth of your time, hooking up a brokerage account to your bank's checking account, and specifying a certain amount of money to flow on a biweekly or monthly basis. Basically, whenever you get a paycheck.

Specifically, $500 per month would max out your IRA eligibility after 11 months, at current contribution limits. Can you follow these steps?

Step 1: Money flows from your bank to your brokerage account.

Step 2: The cash in your brokerage account gets invested according to your automated instructions. This second follow-up step, automating the investment process at your brokerage, we'll talk more about in Chapters 13, 14, and 15.

Step 3: You are wealthy in retirement.

Traditional vs. Roth

Personal finance pundits love to debate "traditional" versus "Roth" IRAs or 401(k) plans. The most important answer, as far as pure mathematics goes, is that:

A.   Don't worry, both are good, and
B.   It's unknowable.

Both are good, because both offer a tax-advantaged vehicle for long-term retirement investing. It's unknowable because we cannot know income tax rates years in the future, when we retire. Mathematical certainty, therefore, is impossible.

The Roth has one or two extra advantages over a traditional IRA, especially for wealthy people, which I'll mention in Chapter 19 on estate planning. It's harder to make Roth contributions, however, as the U.S. Congress has limited eligibility to lower-income limits. If you make a lot of money, they don't let you make a Roth contribution. So, if you can manage to earn little every year but end up very wealthy—a neat and difficult trick—then maybe you'll fully exploit the Roth advantages. My best advice, however, is to mostly ignore the debate on differences and just do your best to make the maximum allowable contribution to either type of account.

THE VALUE OF EARLY IRA INVESTING: OR, AN OUNCE OF EARLY BEATS A POUND OF LATE

Contributions to retirement accounts in your twenties beat contributions in your thirties, forties, and fifties.

If you haven't yet seen this classic comparison of the IRA investments of a 20-something to the IRA investments of a 30-something, you are in for a treat. As with all things awesome in finance, it makes use of the compound interest math we learned in Chapter 4. Also, you should verify this result for yourself in your own handy spreadsheet.

Imagine Sally Squirrel-Nut manages to sock away $5,000 per year to her IRA, beginning at age 22, for 10 years. Then she stops making contributions, after funding her account with $50,000 total. At age 62 she begins withdrawing money to support her retirement lifestyle.

Larry Lateness, by contrast, begins making IRA contributions of $5,000 per year, at age 32. He then contributes the same amount for the next 30 years, until age 61, for a total amount funded of $150,000. At the same age as Sally, Larry begins withdrawing money in retirement.

Who has more money in retirement? We know Sally put in $50,000 over 10 years, while Larry put in $150,000 over 30 years. And yet, in many scenarios, Sally will end up with the better retirement account.

If the IRA accounts manage to compound at 7% annually, Sally will end up at age 62 with $562,582 compared to Larry's $505,365. That's an extra $57,317 for Sally!

If the IRA accounts manage to compound at a higher rate, such as 10% annually, Sally's advantage is even greater, about $1.5 million versus Larry's approximately $900,000, for a difference of nearly $600,000.

This compound interest miracle shows why retirement investing deserves to be an early top priority rather than a later, lower priority of financial planning. This is why you should care about retirement, while still in your twenties, even while still struggling to make your rent.

Could Larry end up better off than Sally in our scenario? Of course. The difference is in the compounding rate. The lower the rate of return, the more likely it is that Larry's account stays larger than Sally's, because the contribution amount, rather than the compounding effect, matters more. If you're curious, the breakeven rate in this particular comparison between Sally and Larry is 6.29%. Meaning, if you can earn a compound rate higher than 6.29% every year, one decade of early contributions beats three decades of late contributions.

How do you get a high rate of return like that? As always, there's no guarantee of any particular investment return, but read Chapters 13 and 14 to give yourself the best chance of attaining that rate or better.

Does It Ever Make Sense to Withdraw Early from a Retirement Account?

This one's easy: no.

The 10% penalty, plus the obligation to pay taxes, plus the injury to your compound interest plan, all make early withdrawals a bad idea. Optional decisions, like withdrawing early to pay for a home purchase, or a to start a business, or to fund educational expenses, or even less worthy purposes like a honeymoon or covering consumption costs, I can't endorse. Don't do it!

Having said that, of course terrible things happen in life such that, while it doesn't "make sense" to withdraw early, many people will do it. And maybe will have to do it.

What I mean by terrible things are death, divorce, impending bankruptcy, impending home foreclosure, an expensive illness, or catastrophic health care costs. For those situations, we're facing a menu of bad choices, for which early withdrawal from a retirement account is just one possibly less-bad option among worse options. I think of all those, however, as forced decisions. At that point, it's not really a choice, but rather something we have to do, regretfully.

Final Thought

My final thought about retirement planning while you are maybe still in your twenties is not about math, but about freedom. I can't prove this mathematically, but you will find your life choices and optimistic outlook enhanced if you have begun your retirement planning early, especially in your twenties. Having a few seeds planted for 50 years of compound interest growth will allow you to make different and better choices to enhance your life.

You can start that business, or get that degree, or take a chance on a move to a new place, if you've already begun to build your own safety net. Flying high and free is better when you have got that underneath you.

CHAPTER TEN

On Taxes

The first rule of taxes is to not pay too much attention to them.

Taxes feel burdensome, high, and un-fun, but they are never the most important determinant of your wealth or poverty. Consequently, taxes should never be the primary reason for making a financial or personal decision.

A simple test in investing, or deciding where to live, or how to run your business, is this: Are you doing it "because of the taxes?" If you answer yes, you are doing it wrong. Taxes are the tail, not the dog. Don't let the tail wag the dog.

You will hear people pitch investments as advantageous "because of the tax loss" like that's some kind of sophisticated approach to money. Investing in loss-making things is not a way to build wealth. Some people justify their overly large mortgage as clever "because I need the tax deduction," which seems like a great way to remain overindebted for life. Some people decide where to live "because of the taxes," which seems as sensible as booking a 5-hour flight across country in order to use the plane's in-flight Wi-Fi. While you should not ignore the effect of taxes on your wealth, you should never justify dumb financial decisions "because of the taxes."

Having said that taxes are the tail, not the dog, being financially savvy means knowing something about how taxes affect us financially. Throughout this book, I mention specific tax advantages of a variety of activities, like retirement savings and investments (Chapter 9), buying houses (Chapter 12), estate planning (Chapter 19), entrepreneurship (Chapter 21), and philanthropy (Chapter 21).

But while those tax tips apply to specific situations, two big-picture tax principles deserve their own chapter, this one. These principles are not "tax tips" as much as they are fundamental and somewhat hidden ways to understand the role of taxes as guardrails on our financial life.

The first point is that income taxes, properly understood, provide a key incentive to saving money. Second, income tax policy in the United States, properly understood, suggests to us something profound about "how to work."

Taxes and Saving Money

On the topic of saving money, taxes are the reason why not only is "a penny saved is a penny got," but also 75 cents saved is equal to a dollar earned. What do I mean by that?

Let's start here: the two basic ways to have more money in the bank are first to earn more, and second, to spend less. A math nerd might express these two ways as:

A.　2 plus 1 equals 3 (earn more), or

B.　2 minus negative 1 equals 3 (spend less)

Taking away an expense, also known as not spending money, gets you that awkwardly phrased "minus negative 1." You recall from your middle school math class that "minus a negative" mathematically is the same as adding a positive.

Anyhoo. The point I'm leading up to is that these equivalent math things *are not treated the same by income tax policy.* Earning money gets taxed. Saving money does not get taxed.

Further, I mean that, in order to put $1 in your bank account, you generally have to earn more than a dollar to obtain it, because the government will take its cut of your earnings, in the form of income taxes. On a larger scale, if you want another $25,000 in your bank account, and you're taxed at a 25% marginal income tax rate, you'll need to earn wages equal to $33,333. With those wages, after you send Uncle Sam his $8,333, you'll have your $25,000. That's a relatively hard way to increase your net worth by $25,000.

By contrast, you can keep an extra $1 in your bank, or $25,000 in your bank, by not spending your money. The choice to not purchase the $1 candy bar at the checkout counter, or to not purchase the $25,000 car at the sales lot, leaves that much cash in your account without paying any taxes on it.

Because of the way taxes affect earnings versus savings, modesty in our consumption—whether candy bars or cars—will keep us on the side of tax efficiency.

Because of taxes, a penny saved is quite a bit more than a penny earned. Saving money is always more tax efficient than earning money. Just something to keep in mind.

Taxes and Work

Understanding the hidden role of income tax policy could influence how you approach the world of work and earning money. Income tax policy in the United States is famously complicated, but I'm going to explain it in simpler terms than I've ever seen it explained anywhere else. Are you ready?

But first, a trigger warning. Depending on your financial situation and political views, this next bit could make you feel queasy. That's OK. The discomfort is normal. Stick with me for a moment.

The U.S. income tax code currently tells us that we as a society reward inheritance the most, followed by living off your pile of wealth next, followed by actually laboring for a living. For most of us, we aren't working in line with the way tax policy is written.

If you inherit money, as of this writing, the first 11.2 million dollars comes tax-free. You owe the government nothing. Under current policy, if you inherit more than roughly 11 million (or 22.4 million if both your parents pass away), then the additional inherited money will be taxed at 40%. What that says to me, and maybe to you, is that the best way to get wealthy in America is to be born into the right family. By "best way" I mean that tax policy rewards children of the very wealthy—at least up to the first 11.2 million—by not taxing their money.

We can debate whether that's "fair" or not. What is clear to me, however, is that tax law rewards inheritance as the single best way to get rich. Perhaps needless to say, this isn't the way the American Dream is typically presented by the Financial Infotainment Industrial Complex. If you think about it too hard, you might get a tad skeptical of the American Dream.

The next best way to get money is by earning interest on municipal bonds, which are typically exempt from federal, state, and city income taxes. If you have $100 million in municipal bonds and you can earn 1% per year on those bonds, you can have that income, that $1 million in annual interest, tax-free. So that's nice, assuming you're already ultra-wealthy.

The third best way to get money, according to the tax code, is from owning businesses that regularly distribute profits in the form of dividends. Dividends are only taxed at 15%, as of this writing, lower than almost anyone earning a living through work, or 20% if you earn a substantial income. What that tells me, and should indicate to you, is that owning a business—or a group of businesses through the stock market, for example—is the next best way to "earn" a living. The tax system rewards wealthy capitalists who can live off their pile of money.

The fourth best way to get money is through long-term capital gains, meaning earning money by buying and selling a stock or business that you've owned for more than a year. If you do this, you will only be taxed at 15%, or 20% if you're in the highest tax bracket. What that tells me, and should tell you, is that the government prefers you to be a wealthy capitalist and earn money through your investment portfolio, rather than through traditional salaried labor. Are you getting the picture yet?

The fifth, and "worst way" to get money, according to the tax code, is to actually work for a living and get paid for that work. If you earn a salary from your employer you will pay, as of this writing, up to 37% on your wages. This tells me, and should indicate to you, that the tax code discourages you from working for your daily bread. Sadly, this is what most of us do. And it's quite taxing.

Again, it's far better, the tax code seems to indicate, to be born wealthy or to live off your pile of investments than to do any work. And again, this is a bit of a departure from the way the Financial Infotainment Industrial Complex presents the American Dream of hard work, discipline, and wealth building.

Hey, don't shoot the messenger. I'm just here decoding tax rates for you.

When I first realized all of this, I'll admit I was kind of upset. Like, that's not fair to the 99% of people who actually, you know, don't have a huge pile of money to keep them clothed and fed. It's not fair to working stiffs who have to go to work every day, rather than just collect tax-advantaged dividends and capital gains, especially on their tax-advantaged pile of inherited money.

I mean, how could the world develop in such an unfair way? Somebody should let the people who write the tax code know what they've done!

Well, Virginia, can you make a wild guess who really writes tax laws in the United States? Also, there is no Santa Claus. We're having this little adult chat because it's enough to make me, or maybe you, think about the injustice of it all. But let's calm down together and make a plan.

Because as my close personal friend GI Joe was fond of saying, knowing is half the battle. If you want to orient yourself most efficiently within the constraints of the tax code as it's currently written, you should consider the value of building up an investment portfolio. You should aspire to put aside money for purchasing assets to provide your income, which will allow you to be taxed at a lower rate than regular working people. You should think about how best to move from earning money as "labor"—taxed at the highest rates, and instead earn money as a "capitalist"—taxed at the lowest rates in our system.

Optimistically speaking, can you move, even if it takes you a slow lifetime, from someone who earns money in a high-tax way—through work—to someone who earns money in a lower-tax way—through investments?

You can bemoan the fundamental unfairness of the tax code. But in the meantime you should also orient yourself to take advantage of it, when and if you can.

Do It Yourself Tax Filing?

Finally, a single word (OK, a contraction of two words) about doing your own taxes: don't.

If you have a job and earn more than a few thousand dollars per year, you can't afford to do your own taxes. A good tax professional will save you time, money, and the risk of running afoul of the IRS.

CHAPTER ELEVEN

On Cars

Can You Buy Your Personality at the Car Dealership?

Let me answer this easy question first: um, no.

The automobile industry, aided and abetted by the advertising world, wants you to think that your car is your personality.

Are you Ford Tough? GM Patriotic? Audi Sporty? Toyota Dependable? Volvo Safe? Mercedes Classy? Lexus Svelte? BMW Engineered? Volkswagen Quirky? Hyundai Thrifty? Tesla Green? I can conjure a car to match each adjective as quickly as I can type the words. I bet we can all match the advertisement to the adjective without pause.

We know that a car is not our personality—our car is a highly engineered transportation machine for moving our physical self from one location to another, on roads. Our car is a modern-day horse, or camel, or ass. Our car is a horse-drawn carriage, pulled by mechanical horses.

The automobile industry would like you to forget that prosaic ass. Instead, folding yourself into the driver's seat—according to the car-industry advertisements—should be a heady combination of comfort, power, and sex.

They want you to think your car will inspire oohs and ahhs. They hope your car makes the neighbors say, like the lady at Katz's Diner says of Meg Ryan in *When Harry Met Sally*: "I'll have what she's having."

Between the airbags and the 0 to 60 acceleration, your car company wants to sell you a Ring of Power, so that you can be the elven queen Galadriel proclaiming, "All shall love me and despair."

The problem is that, despite their advertisements, none of this really happens when you buy a car. The real ass, if you try to buy your personality at the car dealership, is not the one you're riding on.

The more you try to purchase your personality at the car dealership, the more you will pay for something you don't need, and can't buy. This moves you further from the goal of getting wealthy.

On Paying Cash for Your Car

This next bit may not apply to you right now, but for the 5% of you for whom this applies today, and to the 95% of you for whom this could apply some day: you should aspire to pay cash for your car. Some day.

Paying cash at the dealership does two great things for you at the time of purchase and one great thing later.

First, paying cash for your car eliminates a whole series of complicated ways in which a car dealer can fleece you, and we'll talk more about that a little later in the chapter.

Second, paying cash forces you to budget, ahead of time, for your car. Paying cash just might impose some helpful modesty in your purchase.

If you have $10,000 in real cash, meaning actual money in your hand or in your bank when you walk onto the car lot, then you are much more likely to acquire a sensible, boring, used car that you can afford for $10,000, rather than your new, sexy, great-smelling, false personality that the dealer would like to sell you, for $28,000.

The $28,000 new car—of course—you can afford (with those Low! Low! Monthly! Payments!) but also—of course—you don't need.

The difference in this example, at the time of purchase, is that you didn't waste money on a false personality. Rather, you acquired an amazingly engineered machine to move you from place to place. And, you immediately have an $18,000 higher net worth, all as a result of paying cash.

The great optimistic thing later on, for the life of your car, is that you will benefit from the absence of monthly car payments. That means hundreds of dollars, every single month, which you do not owe to anyone. Since we know that the simplest way to become wealthy is to reduce your monthly costs, you will have made a great step toward wealth, by paying cash for your car.

Hundreds of dollars per month not owed to anyone means dozens of hours per month freed up to spend however you like. Or, hundreds of dollars per month can be saved and invested, making you wealthier still in your old age. That's up to you.

Sophisticated Borrowing?

A finance-guy friend of mine told me that it's best to borrow money to pay for a car because a car is a depreciating asset, and we should only pay cash for *appreciating* assets and use loans to pay for *depreciating* assets.

No doubt he could build a probabilistic scenario in which the annual return on his invested capital would exceed the interest rate cost of a car loan, leaving him richer at the end of 10 years by borrowing the money to buy the car.

I'm certain there's some clever financial wisdom in there somewhere, but what works for a sophisticated guy like him is really not the simplest approach for the rest of us. And his financial sophistication unnecessarily violates our core principles, specifically of modesty and skepticism.

The simplest approach, the one most likely to preserve and build your net worth, is to pay cash at the car dealership.

OK, now that I've said all that, I'm almost sorry for this small tangent into the importance of paying cash at the car dealership. I will now return to the real world, as it pertains to 95% of us, right now—and in particular the plain and simple fact that we don't have that kind of cash. We need a loan in order to buy the car.

First: Bring Modesty in Order to Minimize the Merciless Fleecing at the Car Dealership

The first thing to realize when buying a car, on loan, is that you know nothing. Bring modesty to the process.

If you buy a car with cash, by contrast, you don't need to know anything. All you need to know is that you have $10,000 in your hand, and that's enough to get you a fine transportation device. This next part is about the far more complicated process of buying a car with a loan.

You may have spent many days online, researching articles on car-buying tips and with value-comparison mobile phone apps before you walk onto the lot. Good for you, that's better to do than not. But still, you don't know anything compared to the car dealer. I'll explain why.

When you walk on to the car dealer lot you may have the illusion that you're buying a car.

Instead, the reality is that you're simultaneously buying a car, maybe trading in your old car, negotiating a loan, attempting to determine an affordable monthly payment, picking automobile accessories, and discussing dealer warranties and services.

Many of us associate purchasing a car with financial trickery. This association is well earned—indeed the "used-car salesman" stereotype is no accident. But the problem isn't necessarily—or even primarily—the unscrupulousness of the salesperson. I really don't mean to disparage the auto sales industry. They're trying to make a living, too.

I merely mean to point out that this is the largest consumer purchase most of us ever make, and the dealer and salesperson know everything, and we know nothing.

You should understand that with this kind of information and power differential we will not "win" the transaction.

You will do these transactions a few times in your life—maybe one time every 5 or 10 or 15 years. Your salesman from the dealership? He does this multiple times a day. The information and skill disadvantage between you and the car salesman in this transaction is insurmountable.

So first you need to know that you're at a massive information disadvantage. You know nothing compared to the salesman.

Second: Bring Skepticism

Next you need to bring skepticism to each aspect of the car-buying negotiation.

That's because each parallel or simultaneous transaction presents an opportunity, for the car dealer, to get the better of you financially.

The goal for you is not to "win" the transaction, but rather the goal is to get out with a serviceable consumer transportation device with the least amount of fleecing.

When your salesperson tries to combine multiple parallel negotiations into one package—and he will combine these, believe me—you just need to remember that healthy doubt is your friend.

In simplest terms, your best defense is to try to negotiate only one thing at a time, and to understand each step as best you can. The most important negotiation you should actually do ahead of time is to line up a car loan before arriving at the car dealership parking lot.

One Transaction at a Time: Your Car Loan

Here's the question your car salesman will ask when you walk onto the car lot: "Hi folks, how much can you afford to pay per month?"

Big smile. Crinkly eyes. White teeth.

With this seemingly simple, seemingly straightforward question, the car salesman has tilted your head back to better expose your throbbing jugular to his surprisingly pointy canines.

His question is the classic way to combine multiple negotiations without you realizing it.

You see, "How much can you afford to pay per month?" skips over all of the more important questions and negotiations about buying a car with a loan. The important questions should be, in order of importance:

1. The all-in price for your car.
2. The down payment vs. amount of debt on the loan.

3. The interest rate associated with your car loan.
4. The length of time it will take you to pay off your car loan.

By focusing your attention on the monthly payment, the rest of the answers to these questions can be manipulated in the dealer's favor.

Once he knows how much you can pay per month, he can raise the price for the car, raise the interest rate on the loan, and extend the amount of time it will take you to pay off that loan, all of which are detrimental to your personal wealth, but beneficial to his personal wealth.

The simple fact is almost any car loan terms can be made to seem "affordable" if you stretch out the payments long enough. A related fact is that many overly expensive cars can be purchased on credit by manipulating the terms on the loan.

Have you noticed that most automobile advertisements tell you how much per month it will cost to buy or lease the car? No? Well, I hope after reading this you will notice. It's all about focusing your attention on the wrong thing.

Line Up a Car Loan from Your Bank or Credit Union

How do you avoid the canine-teeth-into-your-jugular problem?

The best way, if you need a car loan, is to try to get this loan lined up ahead of time, ideally from your bank or a local credit union.

When you talk to your credit union about a car loan ahead of time, for example, you separate that part of the negotiation from the distracting excitement of obtaining a new vehicle.

Your credit union or bank will want to make money on the loan also, and that's fine, but at least you can review and understand the loan terms—your credit, the loan amount, the interest rate, the loan length of time, the monthly payment—in a quiet, clear manner. Once you have those terms lined up, then and only then is it time to head to the dealership.

As mentioned in Chapter 8, the best kind of car loan from a bank is a low-interest prime loan. If you do not yet have good credit to get this kind of loan, all the more reason to keep your car ambitions extremely modest. A high-interest-rate car loan represents the fast-moving monorail that will keep you poor. If you have to get one, try to keep it as small as possible.

If all goes well, you begin your car shopping at the dealership with a known price limit for your car, a known interest rate, and a known monthly payment amount.

If you got your loan approval ahead of time at your bank, "How much can you afford per month?" is an irrelevant question that you can ignore. You just refocus that salesperson's question back to the all-in price of the car you want.

If—at the end of your car purchase—the dealer can do better than your bank, then so be it.[1] That's great and not uncommon. But the loan negotiation must be kept separate from the car price negotiation, if you want to prevent fleecing.

At the risk of stating the obvious, if you got the best price possible on the car itself and the interest rate is acceptable, then the monthly payment will be fine.

Or it won't. But it will be the best you can get. The bottom line: You should know your acceptable car price and interest rate—based on your income, your credit rating, and the local cost of money—before walking onto the dealer lot.

One Transaction at a Time: The Trade In

When we go to buy a new car, we also frequently muddy the negotiation waters because we have an old car that we need to trade in. This muddying represents another vulnerable point at which we need our skeptical hat firmly screwed to our head.

When we simultaneously trade in our old car to buy a new car, the dealer has the opportunity, for example, to offer us a fabulous (One-Time-Only!) deal on the new car we want, (Saving You Up to $3,000!)—by paying, say, $4,000 less for your old car than what it's really worth.

We may be so sick of the old clunker, and so excited by the shiny new one, that the numbers don't register clearly.

Well, guess what? The numbers register very clearly for your car dealer.

You will probably—although only probably, because I can't be sure on this point—do just as well or better trading in your car at a different used car dealer lot than where you purchase your new car.

You will definitely—and I am sure about this point—do better overall by checking on the value of your used car with other used car dealers apart from the dealer where you purchase your new car. It only stands to reason that multiple potential buyers—if you go to the trouble to check with multiple dealers—enhance the value of your trade in.

Also, you may think it's just plain hard, and annoying, to check at more than one dealer for a price quote on your old vehicle.

But you know what? Being wealthy is hard, and sometimes annoying, and it requires effort. Think of it this way: your car is the single largest consumer item you will ever buy. Unlike almost anything else you could choose to "shop

---

[1]Incidentally, the only relevant way the car dealer should be able to beat your bank is through the interest rate, in other words the "price" of the money loaned. Do not be fooled by some different monthly payment based on an "extended loan," because your bank could also do something like that as well.

around" for, doing the "hard" thing here is potentially worth thousands of dollars to you.

I don't mean to be harsh; I'm just suggesting that if there was ever a time to go the extra mile on negotiating a good deal for yourself, this would be that one time.

If you need to trade in your old car, I understand you may find it most efficient and convenient to drop off and pick up a car in the same place, so I can't frown too much on the practice, for nonfinancial reasons. Creating a true "market" for your used car trade in may seem like more hassle than it's really worth.

However, you should know that the introduction of another moving part to the car-buying negotiation allows for another opportunity for that friendly car salesman to dip into your wallet. Hassles like this are worth thousands of dollars, either for you to keep or the car dealership to keep. It's up to you.

One Transaction at a Time: Cash Back

Car dealerships have gotten in the nasty habit of offering you "cash back," when you purchase a car from them. This cash back deal is a violation of the principle of "one transaction at a time" when car buying. Be very skeptical of cash back offers.

Buying a car "with cash back" means you are doing two transactions:

With cash back you are purchasing your car, as well as taking out an unsecured consumer loan, similar to a credit card advance. You will pay significant fees for this privilege of simultaneous transactions.

Wealthy people do not take cash back from their car purchase, and it's not because they don't need the money. It's because, one way or another, that cash back is a terrible deal for you. If it were a good deal, wealthy people would do it. Wealthy people like cheap money just as much as you. Cash back from a car dealership is the opposite of cheap money.

If you're walking away from a car dealership with extra money cash back following your car purchase, you're doing it wrong.

What about 0% Interest Car Loan Financing at the Car Dealership?

This is the same bad idea here as cash back. File this one under the category: there's no free lunch.

Because we know from our lessons on the time value of money and compound interest (see, if you've forgotten, Chapters 3 and 4) that money today is not the same as money tomorrow, it makes no rational sense, on its face, for a car dealer to offer 0% car loans. And yet, they do this frequently. Why would they do that?

The only way a 0% interest rate car loan makes sense is if the dealer over-charges you for the car. And the overcharging is probably by a significant markup.

Any business that offers you a costly consumer good like a car on credit terms of a 0% loan knows, in their heart of hearts, that they are fleecing you on the price of the car. I don't know if you're overpaying by 15% or by 25%, but you're overpaying.

You have fallen into the trap of conducting more than one transaction with your dealer—buying a car, getting a loan—and the bundling will not work in your favor. It's not much of a clever deal if you get a "great" 0% loan for 6 months but then pay 15% more for the car than you should.

The Right Price for Your Car

I have yet to say anything about what price you *should* pay for your car.

I cannot know—without knowing your whole financial picture—how much you should pay for a car. I do know—without knowing anything about your finances—that you enhance your chances of being wealthy by paying as little as possible for your car.

How can I be so sure of this? Because cars are not investments. Cars are consumer goods.

Unlike say, houses, cars only lose value over time. Cars are big consumer goods that depreciate in value. Buying a new car means you've got 1 day to enjoy your higher value consumer good. After that 1 day, you own a used car. With a significantly lower value once it leaves the lot.

Wealthy people understand that the value of their car the very next day, should they choose to sell, is significantly lower than it was when they bought it the day before.

As a result, all money you put into the car purchase—as well as all money spent maintaining your car—evaporates. You never get it back. Yes, I under-stand there's a special category of collectible cars like vintage Ferraris, but if you're participating in the collectible car world you have too much money—and too little wisdom—to spend time reading this book.

The more you pay for your car, the more money you've vaporized with con-sumption. Since mass model car prices—as of this writing—range from under $10,000 for a used but solid transportation device to around $70,000 for a luxury car with all the trimmings, the most specific I can be is to push you toward the low end of the range. The rest is up to you.

Financially savvy people seek out a used car that scores highly on ConsumerReports.com tests for long-term performance, safety, and low maintenance.

An Optimistic Thought

Finally, here's an optimistic thought. While most of us cannot avoid buying a car, we can determine our loan status ahead of time, we can determine how much we can afford, we can do a tremendous amount of online research into car makes and models, as well as about the accident and repair history of any particular used car on the market, and we can look to save as much money as possible by buying our car.

There's a bit of complexity to the car-buying experience, so let me summarize.

SUMMARY LESSONS:

- You cannot buy your personality at the car dealership. Despite a lifetime of absorbed advertisements, remember that you are purchasing transportation, not sex appeal.
- You have a huge information disadvantage with respect to the dealer, so be both *modest* and *skeptical*.
- An all cash purchase is best, although not always available to everyone.
- Used is cheaper than new, so buy used if you can.
- Focus on the total cost, not the monthly payment.
- Secure your car loan ahead of time to minimize fleecing.
- "Cash back" and "0% financing" are bundled, trick transactions. You are not actually "winning" this transaction.
- Use *Consumer Reports* to determine long-term performance and durability.

CHAPTER TWELVE

On Houses

No other single decision encapsulates the financial opportunity, longing, and anxiety as much as the move from renter to homeowner. That's my excuse for why this is one of the longest chapters in the book.

On houses, everybody has an opinion. Everybody has experience. Everybody is an expert. This is the best financial decision you'll ever make. Houses are a terrible money pit. Buy the biggest amount home you can afford, and you won't regret it. Do not go into too much debt. Borrowing against your home is a savvy financial move. Never treat your home like an ATM.

These contradictory expert opinions are simultaneously correct and true while also being confusingly insufficient. As is the pattern of this book, we need simple rules. We also need our consistent financial attitudes of optimism, skepticism, and modesty to reduce anxiety and do the right thing for the long run.

I will return to the idea—which I deeply believe—that homeownership is the single greatest tool for wealth creation to which a middle-class person has access. An optimistic thought.

I will return to that idea only after first discussing reasons why we should remain skeptical and modest in our beliefs and expectations around homeownership.

You see, homeownership represents at least three functions: necessity, consumption, and investment.

Shelter is of course a necessity, in that we seek a roof, protection from the elements, and a place to store our stuff. A house also represents consumption, in that we can find necessary shelter in a 400-square-foot efficiency apartment, a 4,000-square-foot mansion, or a 40,000-square-foot palace. The differences there partly represent differences in consumption. Finally, a house may be an investment, in which money you put into it may return to you in the future, as more money.

We may muddle these three different purposes of necessity, consumption, and investment when considering a home purchase, but keeping this muddle in mind may help us think more clearly about our decisions.

When you say, or someone says to you, "Well, you have to have a house, so you might as well buy one," that confuses the issue of necessity—the need for shelter—with the choice to invest. When you say to someone, or someone says to you, "Well, I must be in this particular neighborhood or I must have this extra space," that confuses the issue of consumption—a pricey neighborhood or generous square footage—with the issue of investment.

I bring up the necessity and consumption aspects of a housing choice—as distinct from the investment aspect—really to make the following point: you can rent a place to live to satisfy your need for shelter and your need for comfort, and that's a fine choice. You don't have to buy your shelter. For some people and some situations, renting for a lifetime is perfectly fine. You really don't have to invest in your home.

The Skeptical Thought

Since this chapter concerns chiefly the investment side of a housing purchase, let's analyze investing in a home first with a skeptical eye.

Real estate, as an investment, suffers serious flaws.

First, all real estate costs money to own.

Even raw land, at least in the United States, will be taxed. Houses, of course, will be taxed more than raw land, since you will pay a percentage of the value of land, plus the value of the structure.

Houses also cost money to maintain, typically far worse than raw land. You generally have to pay for electricity and/or gas, water and/or sewer fees, without which the house may degrade. Physical things in this world tend toward entropy. Roofs leak. Foundations sag. Paint peels. Wood rots. If the home is in a town with a code enforcement officer, then you need to incur outdoor maintenance costs or face fines for your nasty overgrown lot full of weeds. You get the idea. In investment terms, houses you live in always produce "negative cash flow."

Of course, back rooms and garage apartments can be lent out for long-term rent or Airbnb income, turning a negative cashflow home into a breakeven or even slightly positive cashflow situation. But at that point you're talking about parts of your home that no longer provide you personally with shelter or consumption, but rather a business. That's a fine choice but not the real issue with your "home" as an investment.

If negative cashflow is the first reason to be skeptical about your home as an investment, the next reason is what investors would call "transaction costs." Homes are really expensive to buy and sell, due to all the fees you pay in the transaction. Real estate brokers charge up to 6% of the selling price, not to mention lawyer's fees, title insurance, mortgage underwriting fees, and taxes. You might lose 8% of the cost of your house when you sell, so let's say $16,000 on a $200,000 home. This is a far greater transactional cost than selling the equivalent amount of stock, where you could pay, let's say, $200 on a stock transaction of $200,000 or 0.1% commission "transaction cost." Almost every other type of investment is more efficient in terms of transaction costs than your home.

The Modest Thought

If "negative cash flow" and "transaction costs" should make you skeptical about using your home as an investment, there's a third important fact about your house that should at least keep your investment expectations modest. Namely, there's no particular reason why your house should increase in value more than the ordinary rate of inflation. As of this writing, with around 2% per year inflation in the United States, you should expect your home to increase in value no more than 2% per year, over the long term.

But wait, you say, you know lots of people who have bought a house, only to have it increase in price by 20% in just 2 years! I can't deny that. That happens, sometimes. It doesn't tend to last.

Real estate, like other types of assets, rises and falls in value with animal spirits, changes in interest rates, shifts in geographic preferences, and economic opportunities. Yesterday's skid row may become tomorrow's hipster hangout and next year's high-priced loft area. Prices may jump 10%, and then 10% again. It happens. Real estate prices may also stagnate in your area, not moving up for 10 years in a row. That also happens. Plenty of areas see prices drop by a few percent per year, for years in a row. That happens, too.

Modestly speaking, you should not plan anything beyond the simple rule that over a long run your home could appreciate in value by around 2% per year, or roughly in line with whatever the prevailing rate of inflation is in your area. That's the simple, modest, skeptical truth.

The Optimistic Thought

But wait, what about the optimism?

What about the fact that I said owning your own home is the single most powerful tool available for building middle-class wealth? That's also true. It begins with the 2% price inflation and, paired with key ideas from earlier chapters on compound interest (Chapter 4), automated savings (Chapter 7), low-interest debt (Chapter 8), and taxes (Chapter 10), homeownership makes for an explosively powerful wealth-building tool.

Compound Interest

Let's start with the modest idea of 2% inflation. You bought your starter home for $200,000. Do you know what that will be worth in 30 years, if you stay in your home that long? Well, based on the compound interest math from Chapter 4, we know exactly what the final price of your home should be.

To save your little fingers from having to turn all the way back to Chapter 4, I'll restate the compound interest formula, which tells us what a starting amount of money will grow to, through a known interest rate and a known period of time.

You remember the formula is $FV = PV * (1 + Y)^N$

We want to know the future value, FV, of your house, 30 years from now.

Remember from the math lesson that our starting value, PV, would be $200,000, which is what you paid for the house originally. The 2% rate of inflation is the Y, also known by the different labels as yield, or internal rate of return, or interest rate, or in this case inflation rate. Finally, the N is 30, for the number of years compounding at the 2% rate.

Plugging our house values into the compound interest formula, we learn that the house in 30 years should sell for $200,000 * (1.02)^{\wedge}30$, or $362,272.

Now, $362,000 will buy approximately the same amount of stuff 30 years from now that $200,000 would when you bought the house, so this result may not at first sound so amazing. But the reality of how most people buy and pay for houses over a lifetime actually makes it likely that this growth in price will build you wealth. We have to weave in a few more of our favorite concepts (from earlier chapters!) to see why.

Automated Savings

Approximately two-thirds of homebuyers use a mortgage to purchase their home in the United States, agreeing to pay for a home over a 15- or 30-year time span in fixed monthly payments. The "down payment," or cash needed upfront to purchase a home, typically represents 20% of the purchase price, although sometimes this number could be as low as 10% or 3%, depending on the mortgage program. For our $200,000 home, let's imagine a 20%, or $40,000 down payment.

The monthly mortgage payment, along with taxes and homeowner's insurance, is probably thought of by a homebuyer as a substitute for rental payments.

"I either pay rent, or I pay a mortgage, but either way I've got this top-priority monthly thing I owe to maintain my personal shelter and comfort" is kind of the thought process here.

It turns out that mortgage payments, month after month, year after year, tap into the key psychological trick to saving money—automated payments, as explained in Chapter 7 on saving.

You paid $40,000 upfront for the thing originally, made regular payments for 30 years, and at the end you have a thing worth $362,000. A main "secret" to why homeownership builds middle-class wealth is that we make regular, affordable payments over a long period of time, and little by little we build wealth. We were going to pay our monthly rent pretty much automatically anyway, but instead we paid for the mortgage, pretty much automatically. It doesn't really feel like a choice to make the payment; we *have* to make the payment.

That's the way in which the "automation" of our monthly payment leads to a big long-term outcome. In investment terms, the $40,000 initial thing you bought became a $362,000 thing you own 30 years later, with a lot of afford-able monthly payments.

It sounds kind of dumb and prosaic, but that's it, right there. It's a neat trick.

Low-Interest Debt as an Inflation Hedge

Most home mortgages are, or should be, low-interest debt, like we talked about in Chapter 8. Low-interest debt is compatible, and even helpful, for building wealth.

If you want to go one step further in exploring the positive personal financial role of a home mortgage, let me intrigue you with the following statement: the combination of homeownership plus a mortgage acts as a very powerful infla-tion hedge. By "hedge," I mean finance jargon for protection against inflation.

We already know that the price of your home will likely jump significantly over a long period of, say, 30 years, even at a modest 2% inflation rate. The amount you owe on your mortgage, however, never goes up. In fact, due to inflation, we could say that the amount you owe effectively goes down over time.

Please note that I'm not talking here about paying down the principal on your mortgage, which of course you do over a period of time. I'm talking about the effect of inflation on the value of money, and therefore on the real cost of your mortgage. The effective cost of a $160,000 mortgage is a lot less 30 years from now, after a period of 2% inflation, than it is now.

How much less? I'm so glad you asked, because this is a perfect opportu-nity for using the discounted cashflow math from Chapter 5!

To figure out the equivalent value today of a $160,000 mortgage 30 years from now, we access that formula we learned back in Chapter 5, in the for-mat of

$$PV = FV / (1+Y)^\wedge N$$

We want to know the present value of a future $160,000 mortgage. Our FV is $160,000. Y, the inflation rate, is 2%. N is still 30 years. So we'd solve for the equivalent present value of the mortgage as

$$PV = \$160,000 / (1.02)^\wedge 30$$
$$PV = \$88,331$$

In reality, we would pay down the mortgage over 30 years. But even if we didn't, the mortgage is worth less in today's dollars after a period of even modest inflation. After 30 years, even if you hadn't paid down the loan principal and had simply paid interest on your $160,000 loan, the equivalent value of $160,000 became worth $88,331, or just 55% of its original value. In essence, our mortgage becomes less onerous over time due to inflation. And the more inflation we experience, the more this effect comes into play.

Let me just connect the dots a little bit more explicitly. If you own a home with a mortgage, you have created a simple little inflation hedge with your very own four walls and roof. If the economy experiences 10% inflation for a few years, affecting the prices of everything, you can reasonably expect your house value will also go up by 10% per year. That doesn't necessarily do you any good when you sell the house, because everything costs more. However, with a mortgage that stays fixed in value despite that inflation, your debt becomes relatively easier to pay off.

If we experienced runaway inflation like what happened in Weimar, Germany, in the 1920s or in Argentina and Brazil in the 1980s, rendering our currency relatively worthless, you could still expect your home value roughly to keep up with prices, while your mortgage melts to nothing. When everyone is a paper billionaire due to runaway inflation, your house will be worth many billions, even while you can pay off your mortgage with just a day's worth of wages. Hence, your inflation hedge!

Taxation

At least in the United States, taxes play a big role in making homeownership an important wealth-building tool. Most people know about one type of tax break that makes this true, but underestimate a different, more important, tax break. I'll explain these breaks from least important to more important.

The well-known, but less important, tax break is the mortgage interest tax deduction. Let's say you pay $4,000 in mortgage interest in a year. Let's also assume you are in a 25% income tax bracket. That means that you can deduct, or not pay, taxes on up to $4,000 in income that year, saving you in this example $1,000. That's pretty nice and a good reason to carefully itemize your taxes. If you own a home with a mortgage, go ahead and save that $1,000 and be happy about it.

The far more important but less discussed tax break for homeownership, in my view, is the capital gains tax exclusion. This tax break says that any price gains on your house, up to $250,000, can be enjoyed tax-free.[1] In our example of a house rising in value from $200,000 to $362,000, you might ordinarily expect to owe capital gains tax on the $162,000 rise in value, except for this break. If you owned stock or owned a business that gained $162,000 in value, you might owe 20% taxes on the sale, or $32,400. The home-ownership exclusion, however, saves you the $32,400, which is pretty huge.

Not only that, but if you sell that first house in order to purchase a new house, the $162,000 worth of gains you enjoy tax-free the first time around just get "rolled in" to the new purchase. With your new home, you've reset the amount of capital gains you can enjoy tax-free. It's a repeatable tax break, which is very delightful.

Even more delightful: If you are married, the combined capital gains tax break is $500,000. That, right there, is a main reason why house-value appreciation is the most powerful wealth-building tool available to middle-class people.

All these taxes are subject to change in the future, of course, but for now they represent a huge subsidy for building middle-class wealth.

We've covered the theoretical and attitudinal side of house buying as it contributes to generating wealth over a lifetime. This theoretical side, properly contemplated and understood, will help you make great decisions and build wealth.

However, four practical notes—particularly for a first-time buyer—will also help.

Those four practical topics are square-footage calculations, the importance of location, the question of renting versus buying a house, and the always-tempting notion of flipping houses.

Price per Square Foot

Savvy real estate folks use price per square foot as the basic unit for measuring the relative expensiveness or cheapness of residential real estate. A 1,500-square-foot home that sells for $300,000 could be said to price for $200 per square foot—because $300,000 divided by 1,500 is $200.

---

[1]The fine print: The capital gains tax exclusion law says you have to have lived in the home as your primary residence for 2 of the last 5 years. So it doesn't work for second homes, or rental properties, for example.

Using that measurement you could compare the relative price of a 1,200-square-foot home for $375,000 to a 2,300-square-foot home selling for $500,000. The first home has a price per square foot of $312.5 per square foot, while the second home has $217.4 per square foot. So even though the second home costs a lot more, it's relatively "cheaper" in this basic measurement of the real estate market.

A few words of caution on price per square foot. Like all simple measurements, it lacks subtlety for making a full evaluation of a property. It won't tell you about whether the kitchen has been updated in the past 35 years, or whether there's a garage for parking your car. It won't tell you whether the floor plan or room layout looks like Salvador Dali set it up on a bad day. Naturally, a house with an updated kitchen, a convenient garage-parking space, and a delightful layout should sell for a higher price per square foot than a house without those things. Price per square foot is only the beginning of your financial evaluation of a house you intend to purchase.

The next point is about the single biggest factor that determines price per square foot.

Location

Conventional wisdom in this instance is spot-on when it states that real estate value depends on three factors, and three factors only:

1. Location
2. Location
3. Location

A 1,000-square-foot apartment in Manhattan might sell for, let's say, $800 per square foot. Meanwhile, half a continent away, you might be able to find a comparable 1,000-square-foot apartment—with similar features—for one-fifth of the cost, like $160 per square foot, or even one-tenth of the cost, like $80 per square foot. As shocking as people find those differences, the real estate market is probably not making a mistake here. The houses can't be moved. The difference in price is entirely due to location, not the quality of the shelter itself. Manhattan dwellers, presumably, have the opportunity to earn high salaries to justify the high cost of their housing. The rural Iowa dweller, meanwhile, pays $80 per square foot, commensurate with the aggregate economic opportunity in that area.

As a practical consequence of the location rule, conventional wisdom further posits that a savvy financial purchaser will evaluate the preferred location of a house first, and all other house features only after that. From there follows the rule that you should "always buy the worst house in the best neighborhood," as it holds value through thick and thin financial times. This strikes me as simple, plausible, reasonable advice.

Renting vs. Buying a House

A quick Google search produces many helpful online calculators for comparing the financial choice of renting versus buying a home.

The calculator will prompt you to enter data such as the current price of a home, real estate brokerage costs, the mortgage interest rate, current property tax rates, and expected future home price inflation. Additional financial factors include the likely cost of renovations, repairs, and upkeep, utilities like electricity and water, and homeowner's insurance. Were you to know the precise answers to these questions (Note: You can't know these precisely) the online calculator may provide either an equivalent "rental price" per month you should pay, or the calculator may provide a sense for a "breakeven time" to buy versus rent. For example, the calculator will tell you that given your financial inputs, you would need to own the prospective home for 2.7 years, or 6.3 years, or whatever, to break even with renting.

These aren't terrible tools to use. I'd advocate, however, for a much more skeptical, and simple approach. The online models provide a falsely precise financial result based on a bunch of assumptions about the future (like home price inflation in your area, rental cost inflation in your area, repair costs, and insurance costs) that you simply don't know.

I'd substitute, instead, only one unknowable future data point. Do you plan to live in this house for 5 years or more? If yes, then owning your own home will *probably* work out just fine, as a financial decision. That's not guaranteed, mind you, just optimistically and modestly speaking, it will probably work. If you plan to live there for less than 5 years, conversely, homeownership also might work out for you, but the odds start to tilt the other way. Plenty of people have "made money" owning a home for less than 5 years, but the high transaction costs and uncertainty of real estate inflation make it a less-sure bet.

I know this "5-year rule" may seem overly simple, compared to the sophistication of an online calculator showing rent versus buy calculations. I agree it's simple. But modesty about what we can really know can be helpful when dealing with future uncertainty.

How do I know the 5-year rule works? I don't. I made it up. I just modestly and skeptically propose that it works quite as well as "precise" online calculators, with all their illusion of certainty. Those models remind me of my Wall Street days, an experience from which I developed a smell-test for people simply pulling numbers out of their extremely precise derrières.

Flipping Houses

Finally, four short words about "flipping" houses, or buying real estate with the intent of selling within a short amount of time, for a profit:

Do not do it.

I've known plenty of people who have made money, and even more people who claim to have made money, flipping houses. Heck, I've inadvertently owned a home myself for just a few years and ended up making a good return on my money. Some people even offer real estate courses in how to do this profitably, for a living. Be deeply skeptical of their claims and methods.

In an inflationary real estate market, everybody makes money in a short amount of time—shorter than 5 years—owning a house. Like mushrooms sprouting after a rain, an inflationary real estate market produces many professional "house flippers," convinced that they've discovered this great opportunity that nobody else knows about.

The Financial Infotainment Industrial Complex typically pours unhelpful fuel on this fire as well. Exciting gurus! House-flipping reality TV! Advertising for seminars! House flipping might seem to work for a short amount of time, but it's always a brief window. When the real estate market turns flat or down, those mushrooms shrivel up quickly and die.

Also, when the market turns flat or down, the unscrupulous among us tend to start offering real estate flipping classes to the least sophisticated among us, describing a great opportunity that no longer exists. The teachers of these courses know the opportunity no longer exists. Let's just say that if the opportunity were so great, they would not have time to offer real estate classes; they would just be out making money from the opportunity itself.

Very few of us—and really only those fully dedicating themselves professionally to the task—can sustainably make a living flipping houses through the full ups and down of an economic cycle. Be modest about your capacity to do this with the professionalism it requires for success. A great many more will lose money trying.

PART 4

Moving Along: Now That You Have a Financial Surplus

CHAPTER THIRTEEN

On Investing: Efficient Markets

The greatest trick the devil ever played was convincing us to pay a lot of money for expensive investing expertise.

OK, that's not really the greatest trick. The truly greatest trick has something to do with makeup and changing our appearance, but I can't really recall it all right now. Anyway.

The point is this: you do not need any specialized knowledge to be a great investor. You do not need to work hard at investing. You do not need to be brainy at all. In fact, if ever there was a section in this book in which you need to combine the three key attributes of modesty, skepticism, and optimism—to avoid the investing traps of braininess, hard work, and stress—it is this chapter, and the next.

Your attitudes toward investing will absolutely determine your success. Here's my pledge to you: with little knowledge, and even less work, you can accumulate an investment fortune throughout your lifetime.

I'll start with skepticism in this chapter and then move on to modesty. In the next chapter, I'll explain the importance of optimism. Finally, I'll combine all three with my big two-sentence rule on how to invest at the end of Chapter 14.

Skepticism

My first piece of advice: Start with a significant dash of *skepticism*.

The Financial Infotainment Industrial Complex would have you believe many myths about successful investing, specifically that it:

- Requires extraordinary brainpower and insight.
- Justifiably consumes lots of time and energy.

- Needs constant vigilance.
- Deserves high fees for services, and high pay for practitioners.

As a former Wall Street guy myself, I respect the extraordinary brainpower, hard work, vigilance, and high pay of folks in the industry. Please be skeptical of these myths, however, as they pertain to your own life.

Customers of financial services don't really need any of that. The less brainpower, time, energy, vigilance, and—most importantly—fees you dedicate to investing, I would argue, the better off you will be. You will not only feel better, but you will end up far wealthier in the long run.

I would like you to believe, to know, to trust in your heart of hearts that skeptical voice about the everyday messages from the Financial Infotainment Industrial Complex.

Almost every investment expert you will meet in your life—especially members of the Financial Infotainment Industrial Complex—has something to sell. They became experts *because* they are purveyors of a specific financial product. I don't have an actual product to sell you—besides this book—and that is really the key to why I hope you'll take these ideas to heart. Whether you do or don't is really up to you. If you want to spend more money for a worse product, hey, it's your own dime. I won't be personally affected either way.

More Bad Than Good

I know far more bad ways to invest than I know good ways. I've even personally tried most of the bad ways to invest. For my personal account I've invested in CDs, individual stocks, high-cost mutual funds, raw land, personal loans, limited partnerships, and options. As a professional fund manager or trustee managing institutional money, I've invested in bonds, private equity, auto loans, venture capital, tax liens, seller-financed mortgages, judgments, annuities, REITs, hedge funds, secondary business notes, and defaulted loans. As a Wall Street bond salesman I sold U.S. Treasuries, emerging market bonds, mortgage bonds, CDOs, CMOs, IOs, POs, CMBS, structured derivative notes, convertible bonds, currency exchanges, options, interest rate swaps, and swaptions.

I mention all this just to say that I've bought or sold a wide range of investment products in my life. And yet, for all the complexity and variety that I've seen, there's very little of it that you need to engage with, in order to do well in investing. All you really ever need to know personally is captured in these next two chapters and summarized in the end of the next chapter in two sentences. Simplicity really is better when it comes to investing.

So, stay skeptical.

On Modesty

On the importance of modesty, we need a quick overview of a 20th-century classic book on investing: Burton Malkiel's *A Random Walk Down Wall Street*.[1]

Professor Malkiel's book is worth reading in full, but a brief summary of the biggest idea will get us far enough along on the path to doing the right thing with our own investing.

Malkiel popularized for the investing public the idea of the "efficient markets hypothesis," which posits that the price of a publicly traded asset (like for a stock or a bond, for example) at any moment reflects the aggregation of all known information about that asset. How does that work? As bad news about a company becomes known, demand for the stock will decrease, causing a price drop. Good news, by contrast, will increase demand for the stock, and the price rises.

Now, understand that we don't need any single group of investors or investor opinions or trades to be "right" at any given time. Rather, the market price is an aggregation of everyone's opinions and everyone's trading. As new information becomes known, prices change. If you embrace the efficient markets hypothesis—spoiler alert, I do—then only "insider information," unknown to the rest of investors, could give you an edge when trading stocks over other investors. And for most situations, trading on insider information is illegal, so I can't recommend you try it.

So, what do we do with this hypothesis?

The logical conclusion that proponents of the efficient markets hypothesis draw is that the point of investing in markets should not be to "beat the market," by trading based on our own knowledge. Because the market—as an aggregation of correct and constantly updating prices at every moment—is efficient, it's not really plausible or profitable to try to beat it. Instead, the point should be to join it, and just earn whatever the market returns over time.

Now, an entire genre of financial literature dedicates itself to exploring the limits of the efficient markets hypothesis, with questions like:

1. When it breaks down
2. Whether anomalously successful investors like Warren Buffett discredit the theory by "beating the market" for decades
3. Where pockets of inefficiency exist, and
4. Whether and how it's possible to have an "edge" in investing.

---

[1] For a popular and extremely thorough representation of the "efficient markets hypothesis," which the author dubs "random walk theory," as well as just an overall great book that inspired index investing in the 1970s, I highly recommend Burton G. Malkiel, *A Random Walk Down Wall Street: The Time-Tested Strategy for Successful Investing* (New York: Norton, 2012).

That's fine. In fact, in a meta-sense, being skeptical of the efficient markets hypothesis can even be healthy. If you search hard enough, there are plenty of limits to the hypothesis.

But still. Let me save you the headache. Even if you can find some plausible exceptions to efficient markets, the correct modest approach is to assume the hypothesis is true. Even if you think you can beat the market—and maybe some people can—I'm here to tell you not to try. Maybe some people can because they have access to information that you don't, or they get it faster than others—I'm including both legal and illegal possibilities here—but you, specifically, are very unlikely to get that information. By the time you get your information, the pros have already reacted. Trust me.

Having worked on Wall Street, the astonishing thing about talking to people who have not worked there is how little people understand the combination of brain power and computing power applied to analyzing, buying, and selling investments—every second of the day. Electronic trading reactions happen in milliseconds after the release of information on any given stock. Public markets are far more efficient than most people realize.

So my second piece of advice on investing—stemming from Malkiel's work, but backed up by my experience on Wall Street—is to approach it with an attitude of extreme modesty. You very likely cannot beat the market, and you shouldn't bother to try. In fact, you will make more money—by paying less fees, transaction costs, and taxes—if you give up trying to beat the market.

When I say you should not try to beat the market, I do not mean to imply—at all—that you should avoid the market—the stock market in particular. I do not mean to give you the impression that it's all a rigged game favoring insiders and pros, and that lay people should avoid it.

Nothing could be further from the truth and my views, as I will try to emphasize in the next chapter, on the importance of optimism when investing. Even though the pros are faster than you and me, we still can generate and extract an enormous amount of value by participating in the stock market. In fact, optimistically speaking, there's never been a better time than now to be an amateur investor, if you remain skeptical and modest in your outlook and approach.

Having emphasized the role of skepticism and modesty when it comes to investing, a few more important ideas need clarification before moving on, in the next chapter, to the role of optimism.

Diversification, or Not

Most investment advisers strongly advise diversifying your investments. Most extremely wealthy people, on the other hand, have extraordinary wealth as a result of undiversified investments, usually by owning their own business.

The famously successful investors who built Berkshire Hathaway, Warren Buffett and Charlie Munger, argue that one key to their success over the decades was concentrated, not diversified, investment choices.

So which should you do? To diversify or not to diversify?

While Munger and Buffett did not diversify, and some professional investors do not diversify, they make investing the primary focus of their life. They can conceivably put all their eggs in a few baskets because they deeply understand those eggs and those baskets. That takes a lot of work. In the case of Munger and Buffett, that takes a lifetime of dedication to investing. You cannot replicate their effort and knowledge. You don't need to do this.

If you approach investing with an undiversified approach but an amateurish part-time effort, I am afraid you will end up taking too many risks. Because investing can and should be an effortless activity for the majority of people, a highly diversified investing approach should work best for the majority of people.

For me, the answer is clear, and it stems from a promise I made at the beginning of these chapters on investing. Keep it simple. Do not work hard at investing. Do not apply specialized knowledge. Remain modest in your approach.

To make money with your money in the easiest possible way, you probably want to diversify.

Individual Securities vs. Mutual Funds

Starting from scratch, a blank investment canvas, I'd always advise buying mutual funds—a basket of stocks—rather than purchasing individual stocks. The first reason is that the efficient markets hypothesis posits that you probably won't "beat the market" through your individual stock selection, so probably you're better off just "owning the market" through a diversified mutual fund. Modestly speaking, you cannot know so much more than the rest of the world does about an individual stock, such that it would justify your purchasing that single stock or bond.

I'm not saying you shouldn't ever own an individual stock, but rather that doing so can't be justified by financial theory. If you were given a stock as a gift, or acquired it through inheritance, then by all means keep it and cherish it. If you derive pleasure owning the stock of a company you admire, then that pleasure has a value all its own. No need to sell.

If you seek diversification through a basket of individual stocks—let's say at least 20 or ideally closer to 30 from a variety of different industries—then your individual basket of stocks is a fine proxy for the market and maybe you don't need to purchase a mutual fund either. I'm OK with that approach, too.

Where you might go wrong as a buyer of individual stocks, however, is in believing that by owning just four stocks that you picked, for example, that you've got a good wealth-building plan in place. It might all work out great. It might even outperform a diversified mutual fund. But it might not. I don't think the risks you're taking justify the reward.

Furthermore, with your net worth too closely tied to the fortunes of a small number of companies, you might be tempted to trade too often. You might be tempted to do a tremendous amount of work, researching or thinking about your investments. I know for my part that whenever I've owned an individual

---

ON DRIPs: DIVIDEND REINVESTMENT PROGRAMS

I don't recommend purchasing individual stocks, when compared to the choice to invest in broadly diversified all-stock mutual funds. One exception to this recommendation that I made happily in my own life was for my kids, as an educational experiment. I wanted them to understand the idea of individual company ownership through owning a stock, so I purchased a small number of shares in one company for each of them.

I mention this because a cool, simple, low-cost, and automated way to buy an individual stock is directly from the company itself. Many companies set up a program for individual investors to buy stocks, without using a brokerage company, through a dividend reinvestment program (commonly known as a DRIP). As the name implies, any dividends earned automatically get reinvested in additional shares of the company's stock.

DRIP programs also allow you as an investor to own "fractional shares" of company stock.

What does that mean? It means that if you earned $20 in dividends, but a single stock costs $100, the DRIP program would allow you to purchase 0.2 of the individual stock directly from the company. This is an advantage for the small-time investor—like my children. I'm pretty sure a brokerage company won't let you ever buy a fractional share like this.

Given this combination of low-cost, small-investor orientation, automation, simplicity, and chance to cut out the middleman, you can sort of see why DRIPs appeal to me.

So if you insist on owning individual stocks, check out DRIPs. With a little digging, the "investor relations" portion of the websites of most major public companies can direct you to the administrator of their DRIP programs.

stock that I end up thinking *way* too much about it for my own good. The temptations to trade, or do work, or research the stocks outweigh, for me, any plausible financial benefit from owning individual stocks over a mutual fund.

Active vs. Passive Management

One obvious response to the efficient markets hypothesis is to say that maybe the key to beating the market isn't picking individual stocks, but rather picking individual investment managers who can beat the market. Much of the Financial Infotainment Industrial Complex dedicates itself to raising up, or beating down, supposedly genius investment managers who can do this for you, at a high cost in fees, of course.

This is a psychological challenge, because we want to believe in the potential for genius. And we want to believe that we ourselves can reliably spot genius when we see it.

You can choose what works best for you. For my part, I bring deep modesty and skepticism to the table when evaluating investment managers who purport to beat the market, for a hefty fee. Many managers manage to do it for multiple years in a row, only to underperform in subsequent years. Maybe you'll be lucky enough to choose a manager whose outperformance consistently beats the market and justifies her higher fees.

I just think it's difficult, ahead of time, to know which managers that will be. And that's why we need to remember that past performance is rarely predictive of future results. Those managers who outperform in one financial environment show a pesky habit of underperforming when conditions change.

If you decide to ever do research into the issue of consistent manager outperformance, I don't recommend you reference marketing materials offered by money managers, as they have something to sell. Rather, seek out independent research done by academic institutions on the ability to consistently beat the market.

I am confident you will find that manager "edge" is ephemeral, while fees, by contrast, are forever. I am confident you will find—because every academic study I've ever seen confirms it—that picking managers who consistently beat the market, enough to justify their fees, is a rare feat. If you can find one, somehow, best of luck to you. I'll remain modestly and skeptically over here, seeking out passive, low-cost managers of my money.

CHAPTER FOURTEEN

On Investments: Risky and Not Risky

In investing, your most important decision will be between "risky" and "not risky" assets. Your choosing correctly depends in turn on the extent to which optimism—a key attitude for growing wealthy—guides your approach.

What Is Investing?

By investing, I mean putting money into a risky situation with the hope and expectation that your money will increase over time. Investing is the process of money-begetting-money through cashflow generation, thus igniting the power of compound interest.

When I say risky, I don't include things like a lottery ticket, from which you should reasonably expect to lose all your money. I similarly don't mean risky activity like gambling at a casino, which could make or lose you money in the short run, but in the long run is a game of chance designed to inevitably reward the casino at your expense. If the nature of the risk is speculative and short-term, that also isn't really investing, in the sense that frequently you will lose all or most of your money, even if sometimes you double or triple your money.

One sign that you are speculating rather than investing is your time frame. Are you hoping this purchase will make you lots of money in 6 months? Or 2 years? In my experience, you are probably closer to speculating than investing if that's your time horizon.

A simple dividing line between investing and speculating—the one I prefer—is 5 years. Do you need some of your surplus money back in less than 5 years? If yes, then you should not invest that money. You should save it, in something like a bank account or bank CD. You shouldn't buy real estate, or stocks, or high-yield bonds or any other risky thing with which you hope to make more money. Just sock it away carefully in a nonrisky bucket and you'll have it ready when you need it.

Conversely, do you not need the money returned to you for 5 years or more? Well, then, go ahead and invest it. You may notice that I use a similar "5-year rule" for buying a house in Chapter 12. To the extent that owning a house is an investment, and a risky one at that, the same rule applies.

Ready for the number one key point of this chapter, but a point that you might find hard to swallow?

Money in your retirement account, by definition money that you hope will last you the rest of your life, should all be invested in risky assets.

What? Huh? You weren't expecting that. But it wasn't a typo. So to be clear about its importance I'll just repeat it. All of your long-term investments, especially retirement money, should be in risky assets.

It should not be in cash, or CDs, or bonds, or annuities, or any safe, nonrisky assets. Purchasing nonrisky assets is not investing. Nonrisky assets are for saving money.

Either Risky or Not Risky

The Financial Infotainment Industrial Complex would have you believe in many different types of investments. That's wrong. Be skeptical. There are only two types of assets: "risky" and "not risky."

Risky assets include stocks, all real estate, private businesses, limited partnerships, commodities, currencies, high-yield and emerging market bonds, and even more exotic products beyond these.

Not risky assets include cash, checking and savings accounts, CDs, highly rated government bonds, highly rated corporate bonds, annuities, and similar products.

Assets cannot be in both categories at once.

Incidentally, be deeply skeptical of anyone trying to tell you that their investment opportunity is both risky (often also described as "high-return" or "high-yield") and not risky. If that's the pitch, you are being sold that asset by a liar or a dupe. Legitimate high-return or high-yield assets are always risky, full stop. Nonrisky assets do not offer high returns, full stop.

One of my pet peeves with a product like a variable annuity is that insurance salespeople try to claim that it offers both high returns ("risky!") but limited downside ("not risky!"). What it instead offers is an illiquid garbage product that pays the salesperson big commissions, charges you huge fees, and as a result, offers you a limited return. Stay away from products like variable annuities that resist categorization as either risky or not risky. All legitimate assets can be categorized as risky or not risky, but never both.

The big question to answer is: How do you decide the right mix between risky and not risky assets? On any given day, the Financial Infotainment Industrial Complex advocates strong reasons to purchase risky, or not risky, assets. On Wall Street, we note this barrage of opinions as the unending epic struggle between fear and greed, and it drives the short-term prices for all assets.

To settle the correct answer to that question requires us to zoom out of our focus on hourly, daily, or weekly changes in market prices, and into the longest time frame possible.

Professor Jeremy Siegel, author of the personal finance classic *Stocks for the Long Run: The Definitive Guide to Financial Market Returns and Long-Term Investment Strategies*, built the time series that helps us see the big picture of long-run returns when it comes to risky versus not risky assets.[1]

Siegel's comprehensive time series focuses on stocks and bonds (and gold), but I think you should consider these results as indicative of other categories of risky and not risky investments. Real estate and private business ownership returns, as risky category investments, might perform roughly similarly to stocks, although understand that the "stocks" data comes from "the entire market," which is obviously more diversified than any individual business or real estate investment property. Savings accounts, CDs and annuities, as not risky investments, might perform roughly similarly to bonds. Gold is not a real investment so has no equivalent, except maybe goofy collectibles like beanie babies or baseball cards.

If you had invested $1 in stocks in 1802, that dollar would have grown to $13.48 million by 2012. A $1 investment in bonds would have grown to $33,992, while an investment in gold would have increased to $86.40 over that time period. These are not trivial differences. In addition, the returns do not favor one time period over the other. They hold true even if you only examine any 50-year period between 1802 and 2012, although with less dramatic monetary outcomes because of the shorter time for compound interest to work.

Those differences are shocking, but should make sense if you've absorbed the astonishing power of compound interest, explored in Chapter 4. Those differences in outcomes are so phenomenal that they blow away any long-term

---

[1]Long-term returns data on different asset classes come from Jeremy Siegel, the author of the classic book: Jeremy Siegel, *Stocks for the Long Run: The Definitive Guide to Financial Market Returns and Long-Term Investment Strategies* (New York: McGraw-Hill Education, 2014), 5–19, 75–85, 133–142.

doubts you should have about the prospects of stocks versus bonds, not to mention, obviously, gold.

Now wait just a minute, you're thinking. What about inflation? That's an important question and one that Siegel addresses. When we adjust for inflation, we talk about "real" returns on investments rather than "nominal" returns.

So here are the "real" returns. If you had invested $1 in stocks in 1802, Siegel reports, that would have grown to $704,997 by the end of 2012. A $1 investment in bonds, by contrast, would be worth $1,778. A dollar invested in gold, for comparison's sake, would be worth $4.52 in real terms.

As we can see from these results summarized in Table 14.1, that is also an extraordinary beat-down by stocks when compared to bonds over the long run. And gold is basically just pathetic, hardly even worthy of mention.

I hope you can see that this isn't a fair fight between stocks and bonds, when considered over the long term.

Another way of comparing stocks and bonds, or risky versus not risky, is through looking at their respective accumulated percent annual returns. Because we live in the real world, the best comparison takes into account both inflation and taxes, so we need a "historical asset real return, after taxes" number for stocks and bonds (and gold).

Table 14.2 shows returns from 1802, as well as returns from 1871, 1926, and 1946 until 2012. The more recent time periods highlight the effect of increasing taxes (the U.S. national income tax started in 1913) and the effect of inflation (which ramped up in the 1960s). This data assumes an investor in the highest tax bracket.

Table 14.1 Stocks vs. Bonds: The Long-Term Growth of $1

What $1 Invested Becomes from 1802 to 2012	Nominal Growth	Real Growth
Stocks	$13.48 million	$704,997
Bonds	$33,992	$1,778
Gold	$86.40	$4.52

Data above from Jeremy Siegel, *Stocks for the Long Run: The Definitive Guide to Financial Market Returns and Long-Term Investment Strategies,* 5th ed. (New York: McGraw-Hill Education, 2014), 5–7, 75–92.

Data on Nominal Growth from "Figure 5-1, Total Nominal Returns and Inflation, 1802–2012," Siegel, 77.

Data on Real Growth from "Figure 1-1, Total Real Returns on US Stocks, Bonds, Bills, Gold, and the Dollar, 1802–2012," Siegel, 6.

Table 14.2   Historical After-Tax Real Annual Return on Investment, 1802–2012

Historical % Real Returns After Tax	1802–2012	1871–2012	1926–2012	1946–2012
Stocks	5.0%	4.1%	2.8%	2.8%
Bonds	2.4%	1.2%	−0.2%	−1.0%
Gold	0.7%	1.0%	2.1%	2.0%

Data shown assumes highest federal income tax bracket, and 1-year holding period for capital gain portion of return. After-Tax Real Returns on stocks, bonds, gold, from Jeremy Siegel, *Stocks for the Long Run: The Definitive Guide to Financial Market Returns and Long-Term Investment Strategies*, 5th ed. (New York: McGraw-Hill Education, 2014), 133–142.

The key takeaway from these percent annual returns is that the real after-tax return on risky stocks overwhelms that of not risky bonds, when you take the long-run perspective. Remember from the math of Chapter 4 that small differences in percent annual return make for extraordinary differences in the long-term compound growth of money.

Those numbers indicate to me that stocks so far outperform bonds over the long run that a reasonable person trying to build wealth could hardly consider bonds as a viable alternative. Stocks, viewed in the short run, appear risky, while bonds by contrast appear not risky. But Siegel's data corrects that view. The real return on not risky bonds, taking into account inflation and taxes, is negative for approximately the last century. The real return on risky stocks, taking into account inflation and taxes, is consistently positive.

I think we need one more set of numbers to convince us of what's right. You may have doubts about this ultra-long-term perspective because none of us actually get 200 years to invest. If you're just out of college, you have maybe 50 years to invest. If you start investing when most people start investing, you will have less than 30 years to invest. So what are the prospects for risky versus not risky with the more limited time of actual investors?

Here, too, the evidence for the outperformance of stocks versus bonds is convincing. Despite the volatility of risky stocks in the short run, the longer you hold them, the more likely it is that volatility will cease to matter because the returns on risky stocks beat not risky assets like bonds.

David Hultstrom of investment advisory Financial Architects LLC provides the data in Figure 14.3 that shows the likelihood that stocks outperform bonds for different historic holding periods. Meaning, what are the odds of winning with risky investments instead of not risky investments, and how do they shift over longer and longer periods of time?

Table 14.3   Historic Probability That Stocks (U.S. Total
Stock Market) Beat Bonds (5-Year Treasuries), 1926–2016

Number of Years Held	% Probability That Stock Returns > Bond Returns
1	64%
5	70%
10	80%
15	87%
20	99%

Data from David Hultstrom, Financial Architects, LLC. Used with
author's permission.

In any given 1-year period between 1926 and 2016, stocks beat bonds 64%
of the time. For this and other reasons, you can't put all your money in the
stock market if you need your money back after just 1 year. Over a 5-year
period, however, stocks beat bonds 70% of the time. For investments held for
10 years, risky beats not risky (aka stocks beat bonds) 80% of the time, while
15 years gets you to a nearly 90% probability. Over a 20-year period, Hultstrom's data shows, you're up to a 99% or more probability that risky will outperform not risky. We haven't seen bonds beat stocks over 20 years, between
1926 and 2016. For me, this kind of data takes Siegel's long-term information
and brings it down to the time frame in which we actually live.

There's an even clearer way to think about these probabilities. If you choose
to invest in bonds over stocks in a long-term portfolio like a retirement account,
you are essentially betting that the lowest probability thing is going to happen.
You are saying "it's different this time," which is a classic investing mistake.
You are betting with your own money that some extremely improbable thing is
likely to happen, the visible odds and historical record be damned. That seems
to me like a particularly immodest way of approaching investments. You are
making a foolish and—dare I say it—risky bet that is unlikely to pay off.

Once you see the long-term data, properly understood, what exactly is risky
and not risky in the investment world?

The Power of Optimism

Nowhere in your financial life is the role of optimism more powerful in
generating wealth than in the choice of whether to invest in risky assets like
stocks instead of not risky assets like bonds.

Biologically speaking, our brains evolved to seek out risks that exist in the
current moment, rather than calmly conceive of probabilistic risks as they
develop, or don't develop, over decades. As a result of our brain wiring, we

have to intentionally block out the minute-by-minute and day-by-day noise about a risky world—as pushed by the Financial Infotainment Industrial Complex—in order to do the right thing. My shorthand word for this blockage is—

Optimism.

Investing in risky assets, primarily stocks, in the long run, will all work out.

It's easy to forget that the long-term returns of stocks, since 1802, or 1926, or 1987, or virtually any long time period you pick didn't seem preordained, or obvious, or even likely, at the time. At any moment in time the stock market either looks risky because it just went down, or overly complacent because risks loom on the horizon and yet prices are stable, or like a bubble because it has gone up so much recently and it's bound to crash.

One of those three messages I just described above is literally the message of the headline of the *Wall Street Journal* today, and every day, since I began subscribing 20 years ago. And that's not the worst newspaper about financial markets. It's the best. It's not wrong in the short run. It is wrong in the long run. In the long run, the stock market goes up.

If you think the best stock market returns are all in the past, when the "easy money" was made, and that from here on out it will be much tougher, then you are forgetting about history. In particular, you are forgetting just how horrible things were when the stock market offered incredibly good long-term, real, after-tax returns on investment.

Like the 1914–1918 period, when the richest countries in the world destroyed a whole generation of men in World War I. Or the flu pandemic that followed in 1918, killing another 50 to 100 million people, or 3% to 5% of the world's population.

Or when virulent, violent, and eventually totalitarian communism took over one of the emerging global powers, Russia, in 1918, and retarded private market growth there for the next 80 years.

Or when fascism infected Italy, Germany, and Japan in the 1920s and 1930s, plunging the entire planet back into World War II, causing another 50 million deaths and the destruction of the productive capacity of Europe and Japan.

Or when the United States and Russia faced off in an arms race for 40 years, threatening the planet with mutually assured nuclear destruction and fighting proxy wars in developing countries.

Or when the oil shortages and embargoes of the 1970s combined with high inflation, price controls, and high taxes in the United States to return an aggregate of around 0% on stocks between 1968 and 1982.

Or when the 9/11 attacks and other terrorist attacks on civilian targets—combined with U.S.-led never-ending wars in Iraq and Afghanistan—increased uncertainty around the world in what appears to many as a clash of civilizations.

Throughout those events, each of which felt like an existential threat to life as we knew it, the stock market kept chugging along. Not only chugging along, in fact, but producing wealth, technology, and medical gains that dwarfed the preceding millennium's progress.

In 1850, the life expectancy at birth of someone who looked like me, a white male in the United States, was 38.3 years. That increased to 48.2 years by 1900, just 50 years later. By 1950, following some of the world's worst catastrophes, life expectancy for someone like me increased to 66.3. At the time of this writing, a white male child born in the United States has a life expectancy of around 76.3 years.

As a consumer of media, you may sense on a daily basis that everything is heading for a complete catastrophe, and I don't blame you for thinking this. But the evidence based on life expectancy alone points otherwise. And the pace of technological improvement is not slowing: it's increasing.

One simple way to understand this disconnect is to know that the Financial Infotainment Industrial Complex does not get paid to tell us good news. Good news does not generate clicks and eyeballs and all the things advertisers want. Yet, from a technology, wealth, human health, and productivity perspective—the stuff that drives returns on stocks over decades—we've experienced unrelenting good news.

Just like you, I don't spend my day wandering around smiling broadly like a crazy loon because of all the good news. Most days, I'll admit, the bad news grabs 98% of my attention. But the reality over decades of human progress is that progress not only occurs, but it also accelerates.

If you insist on investing with the attitude that the good times are in the past, that "this time is different," just understand that you've broken a cardinal rule of investing.

The only attitude that makes any sense is that this growth in technology, health, wealth, and productivity will keep on going. As financial adviser and author Nick Murray says succinctly in his excellent book *Behavioral Investment Counseling* (and whose writing frankly inspired this last section on human progress), "Optimism . . . is the only realism."[2]

100% Risky for the Long Run

Siegel's conclusion to his book on the long-run prospects for stocks, taking all this into account, is that rational investors who want to build their wealth should seek to own a long-term portfolio of 100% stocks. Because of

---

[2]On the power of optimism and the incredible technological improvements and wealth creation of the modern era, I owe a tip of the hat to Nick Murray, *Behavioral Investment Counseling* (New York: The Nick Murray Company, 2008), 60–69.

the historical outperformance of risky over not risky assets, despite differences in volatility, he says that a greater than 100% allocation to stocks—up to 134% of your portfolio—would be rational for a 30-year holding period or longer. Greater than 100% is not available to the average investor—you could do this through borrowing money or alternative investments like hedge funds, although I won't endorse either of those for the average individual investor—but his point still stands.

The power of compound interest works so much more strongly on stocks than bonds that a choice to favor not risky assets like bonds makes little sense, if you maintain the long-term view.

The Special Case of Gold

I have not lumped gold into the risky or not risky categories above, even though parts of the Financial Infotainment Industrial Complex would have you believe in the importance of gold as a "store of permanent value," or "hedge against inflation." That's because gold is not an investment at all but rather a psychological trick played on the financially naïve by fear-mongering promoters and their pseudo-analyst enablers. Gold generates no cashflow and therefore will never benefit from the power of compound interest. Gold is just a collectible lump, as valuable in any given year as other financially naïve people want to make it. Its long-term returns are catastrophic, yet it provides little medium-term or short-term safety because its price can be quite volatile. All I can really say about gold is that it has no place in your financial portfolio.

Arguments against 100% Stocks

If you do endorse the all-risky portfolio, know in advance that this only works out well if you resist the temptation to sell when the market goes down. An all-risky portfolio creates the most money in the long run, but will endure huge swings up and down in the short and medium run. For that reason, few investment advisers actually allow their clients to invest in all-risky assets, despite their obvious, overwhelming advantage in the long run.

Josh Brown, a writer and investment adviser known to his fans as "The Reformed Broker," makes a great case against a total reliance on stocks in an investment portfolio.[3] At the same time, he also makes the case that readers of this book should recognize as points in favor of an all-stock portfolio.

---

[3]Reasons to avoid a 100% stock portfolio from Josh Brown. "Should You Be 100% Long Stocks." Accessed September 1, 2017. http://thereformedbroker.com/2016/02/13/should-you-be-100-long -stocks.

Arguing that 100% is generally inappropriate, Brown mostly tongue-in-cheek mentions five scenarios in which an investor could build a 100% stock portfolio:

- The investor is under 35 years old, starting from a small base, and is automatically dollar-cost averaging every month.
- The investor is in a coma of an indeterminate length.
- The investor has been diagnosed with a terminal disease and is going to be passing on the assets to the next generation soon.
- The investor's portfolio is very small in comparison with their other assets, assets that are not fully correlated with stocks.
- The investor is going to be living on a desert island for two decades without access to TVs, radios, the Internet, or Barron's.

Brown's first scenario is in fact precisely who this book is written for. Scenarios two and five merely point out—in my mind—that the Financial Infotainment Industrial Complex described more fully in Chapter 2 does not help you build long-term wealth, but rather hinders, frightens, and distracts you. Scenario three in fact makes the case indirectly for conceiving of stocks as a way to build intergenerational wealth for the longest time horizon. Scenario four is a way of saying that having undiversified exposure to stocks will be a bumpy ride. Which I agree with, but I still would advocate "all risky" as well worth it.

In the next chapter I argue that you probably need an investment adviser to help you as a copilot to weather that bumpy ride. And if that copilot keeps you on course through market volatility, he or she will have been worth every penny.

So here is the only two-sentence rule on investing you need to know, in order to invest well:

Regularly purchase low-cost, diversified, 100% stock mutual funds (probably indexed), and never sell. Ninety-five percent of you should do this, with 95% of your money, 95% of the time.

If you remain uncertain, even after reading this book, what any of those terms mean, just bring the first sentence to your investment adviser and say "I want this, and only this." Your investment adviser may object, since it very likely doesn't follow what he or she would plan for you. Just trust me. Remember, I'm not making money off you either way. Unlike everyone else in your life, I don't benefit in any way from your decision.

Notice I've left a little wriggle room. Do you like to buy individual stocks? Go ahead and do this with less than 5% of your money, and you'll be fine. Just know that the 5% activity is really your own investo-tainment and shouldn't have much effect on your personal wealth. Do you want to get into more exotic investment products? Fine. As long as you limit yourself to 5% of your investible funds, I can't fault you too much.

Caution!

A 100% risky portfolio is the best way to build wealth in the long run. However, this deserves a word of caution, previewed above by Josh Brown's wise words. A 100% risky stock portfolio only works to build wealth if you never sell. This is so important it needs to be said again. You cannot sell when the market goes down. You cannot sell because you have a hunch that financial trouble is on the horizon. For this plan to work, you have to buy and hold no matter what the Financial Infotainment Industrial Complex tells you is going on. Most of us are not strong enough to never sell. Which is why, in the next chapter, I explain that most of us need a financial adviser.

CHAPTER FIFTEEN

On Investment Advisers

So let's say you managed to wrestle down your high-interest debt to nothingness (Chapter 6), and you've conquered the problem of acquiring savings on a monthly basis (Chapter 7). Hopefully you've made some decisions around starting a retirement account (Chapter 9) and around buying a home (Chapter 12). You've begun your investment journey (Chapters 13 and 14), managing to scrape together somewhere between $25,000 and $25 million. Likely closer to the former number admittedly, but hey, I'm an optimist.

Around this time, you will confront that age-old question of the bourgeoisie: Do I need an investment adviser?

The quick answer, modestly speaking, is that 95% of us do.

The longer answer, which takes up the remainder of this chapter, is why you probably need one, what an investment adviser should do, how to find one, when you should fire one, and how you would know if you're in the 5% category that doesn't need one.

So Why Do You Need an Investment Adviser?

Let's start with the wrong answers.

Your adviser beats the market. Your adviser has unusual insight into market values, trends, and patterns. Your adviser has special access to deal flow that other people do not have. Your adviser has computer software that can give him, her, or you, an edge. Your adviser is a friend of your uncle, and you should go to him. Your adviser is a great golfer, and you do love golfing.

All of these reasons are just plain wrong. About the first few claims—to special insight, technology, or access—I can only urge you to put on your most skeptical goggles and resist the temptation to believe this bunch of lies. The last few reasons—having to do with relationships and nonfinancial expertise—are less wrong, but might lead you to settle for less than the best investment adviser for you.

We are also, incidentally, beginning to answer the question of how to find an investment adviser. An adviser who talks about the great return he or she can get on your money is not the right one for you. I know that sounds a bit contrarian, but just stick with me for a bit here. An adviser who spends the bulk of the "getting to know you phase" focused on golf outings and NBA tickets probably will not serve you best in the long run.

Now pay attention closely to this next part, as it's the key point of the chapter.

A good investment adviser has two, and only two, functions: the "plan" and the "hand."

First Function: The Plan

First, your investment adviser should get to know your specific financial situation well enough to design a simple, foolproof, automated, all-weather plan for you. This plan design may take a few hours of discussion, but it should not take a professional much more time than that.

A good plan primarily consists of setting up a sensible asset allocation to fit your longest-term wealth goals. It will include provisions to periodically rebalance your allocations.

If you are still in the wealth-accumulation phase of your life, that good plan will also include automatic contributions from your paycheck or savings account into your investment accounts, without you having to make the decision to automatically contribute. This automation, as discussed in Chapter 7, is absolutely *the key* to a good plan.

A sign of a good plan is not how it performs when the investment adviser and you are "right" about the markets. Rather, a good plan is one that performs to expectations even when you are totally "wrong" about the markets, or the markets "misbehave."

So Which Asset Allocation Should the Plan Have?

Careful readers of Chapters 13 and 14 will already know what I consider the correct asset allocation for a person still in the wealth-accumulation phase of life. I am realistic enough to know, however, that your investment adviser will instead design a plan consisting of roughly 60% stocks and 40% bonds. Because they all do. That's fine.

Here's my cynical view of why the 60/40 split is where advisers all end up. It's so that when the market goes down by 35% next year, they can point to the solidity of the 40% allocation to bonds and show how prudent they were all along. That way, you won't fire them in the midst of the downturn. It's a client-retention strategy. Even though, as you know from the previous two chapters, it's holding back your wealth accumulation pretty significantly.

So, I don't agree, but I understand. That's between you and your investment adviser. At this point the key is that you make a plan and that you decide with your investment adviser to stick with whatever you decided together. Especially for the next function of the investment adviser: the hand.

Second Function: The Hand

When the financial markets next crash by 35%, the role of your investment adviser is to hold your hand, patting it occasionally, for comfort. This has the effect, hopefully, of calming your nerves. In addition, the good adviser is also firmly holding your hand in place to prevent you from doing anything rash.

Do not sell. Do not trade. Don't press that button. Don't call up your broker. Don't stop automatic contributions. Do not change your asset allocation targets in the middle of a crash. This is not the time go into safe assets. Stop! The adviser's grip on your hand needs to be quite firm indeed.

Your investment adviser, a good investment adviser, is there to grab your hand and prevent you from doing the wealth-destroying thing, which would be to deviate from your initial plan in the midst of the market crash. Your investment plan only works if you continue to contribute the same amount, despite the 35% crash, and despite the fact that it looks like the world is ending. By the way, the world is not ending.

Incidentally, your investment adviser needs to be optimistic about the long-term power of investing. Optimism is the key to easy, long-term, wealth accumulation.

Here again, we are partly answering the question of how to find the best investment adviser.

When interviewing an adviser, you should ask what they would do to avoid a 35% loss on your equities investment.

Note: This is a trick question. The correct answer is that the 35% drop in the market is not avoidable. He or she can't time it right, avoiding the crash ahead of time. If your adviser claims to be able to time it right, to be "nimble" and ready to "trade around" in the face of a declining stock market, you are talking to a liar or a confused person. He or she is ignoring (or worse, hiding) all the research that's ever been done on "timing" the market.

You should also ask what he or she intends to do with your equities portfolio after the market drops 35% (which I'm telling you right now, and they should have told you from the beginning, they were unable to avoid). This is also a trick question. The correct answer is: nothing. Do nothing. The adviser's role is to pat your hand reassuringly, and then to grip your hand to prevent you from selling.

A good investment adviser knows that a 35% drop doesn't mean the stock market is broken. Stock markets drop by 35% every decade or so. It's just what risky markets do. The good investment adviser knows that regular automatic contributions to your portfolio—especially after the 35% drop in prices!—are the absolute key to accumulating long-term wealth. This is known as dollar-cost averaging. Remain optimistic after the crash. This is how you will gain wealth in the long run.

So how do you know if you're in the 95% category of people who need an investment adviser?

You should ask yourself two questions.

First, do you know how to set up a simple, automated, all-weather asset allocation investment plan at a reasonable price that will work even if you're completely wrong about what will happen in the future? Be modest here. It's OK to need help. If you're not sure of the answer, you need an investment adviser.

Second, do you know *with 100% certainty* that you will stick with that original all-weather plan when all the world falls apart? Again, be modest and skeptical about your stick-with-it-ness. The Financial Infotainment Industrial Complex (remember Chapter 2!) will try to convince you that "this time is different" and that you need to break with your plan. If you're not sure if you will be tempted by those voices of madness, then you need an investment adviser to hold your hand. If you have managed to survive a major downturn already in your life without changing course, then perhaps you do not any longer need an investment adviser.

Firing Your Adviser

I hope you can read between the lines about what kind of investment adviser should be fired. Anyone who claims unusual expertise or an amazing track record should be viewed with deep skepticism. I've met a tremendous number of smart finance and investment people in my life, but I've never personally met someone who I would trust if they told me they could consistently "beat the market" by managing my money. I'm not saying it's impossible. I'm just urging profound skepticism.

Remember, your investment adviser's role is not to "beat the market," but rather to set up a reasonable plan and then to hold your hand.

While 95% of people with $25,000 or more in investible assets probably do need an adviser, over time some smaller number of people need that adviser for the rest of their life. What I mean by that is that more than 5% of people can do it themselves, after some years of having an investment adviser. Optimistically I think that after 5 or 10 years of paying an investment adviser, lots of people could take on managing their own money. After 20 years, you'll probably have been through a significant market blow-up, and you'll know how it feels. Did you panic? Did you sell? Did you change your asset allocation when the Financial Infotainment Industrial Complex told you "this time is different"?

If you stuck to your plan after the stock market fell 35% percent, then you might be ready to graduate to managing your money without an investment adviser. If you are not absolutely sure of how you'll react, however, you will be better off continuing to pay a good investment adviser, even though all they are doing is telling you to "stick to the plan" when you're totally panicked.

Fees

Finally, let's talk fees. A reasonable investment adviser charges 1% of the value of your assets per year. So to be concrete, you should happily pay $1,000 per year on your $100,000 portfolio. If you have a large investment portfolio, you will pay a lot more money than that to your investment adviser, since 1% of a larger portfolio can get pretty large. If you and your investment adviser designed the foolproof plan, and he or she prevents you from being a fool when the market crashes, the 1% per year will be well worth every single penny.

If you do some compound interest math on the effect of that 1% fee over a lifetime of investing, you will be shocked to discover that your investment adviser might capture 20% to 50% of your investment gains. Fees well above 1% per year, for 40 years, will start to approach closer to 50% of your investment gains, whereas a lower fee for fewer decades will capture your gains at the bottom end of the range. For even a normal-sized investment portfolio, you should expect to pay tens of thousands to hundreds of thousands of dollars to your investment adviser.

These numbers, added up over the long run, are in fact stunning. That's why I'd urge you to evaluate after 5 or 10 years whether you are ready to graduate to running your own money, by reviewing those initial questions above. But be brutally honest with yourself. If you don't know for sure, you need to keep your investment adviser. Panicking mid-crash, or failing to automate, or generally stressing about the ups and downs of investing, can and will cost you more than 20% to 50% of your investment gains.

CHAPTER SIXTEEN

On Insurance

Here's the most important rule on insurance:

Insurance works *only* as a financial risk transfer.

As a result, the single question you must always ask when buying an insurance product is this:

What financial risk am I transferring from myself to the insurance company that I can't get rid of in any other way?

If you can answer that question clearly and concisely, then you should go ahead and purchase insurance for that risk.

Here are good examples of personal financial risk transfers for which you probably do need insurance:

- You negligently hit somebody with your car, making you personally liable for the harm done.
- Your house's roof collapses when an old tree falls on it, making it necessary to rent a different house while you rebuild the roof, or rebuild the house, or buy a new house.
- You become physically or mentally incapacitated and can no longer earn an income sufficient to support yourself or your dependents.
- You or your loved ones require expensive medical care.
- You die, with children too young to have completed their education.

Each of those events, though relatively rare, may cause a catastrophe for which few people are financially prepared. Auto, homeowner's, disability, health, and life insurance can transfer these rare but catastrophic financial losses away from you personally and on to a big corporation. You should pay money to the insurance company to transfer those risks. Even if you never end up needing the insurance, you can be happy to have had the risk financially removed from you and put onto that company.

I know many bad types and uses of insurance, however, so the thrust of this chapter is to warn you against buying too much unnecessary insurance.

The marketing folks of the insurance industry would like to fog up the answer to my single question about risk transfer. The insurance industry would have you believe that risk transfer goes together with things like investments and emotions and safety blankets, in a nice big comfortable package. Remain skeptical.

"Let me sell you this fuzzy blanky comforter," the insurance salesperson says, attempting to tuck you into a nice annuity product that provides steady income without risk. "You are a child," the insurance marketing seems to whisper into your ear, "and you deserve a fairy tale full of unicorns and rainbows. Investments and risk transfer snuggle up together in the comfiest way."

That, right there, is a garbage-filled fairy tale clogging up your financial future. It has funded the construction of the tallest buildings in your city— usually owned by insurance companies. Don't be a child, and don't believe it. Don't pay too much for too much of a safety blanket. Investing most definitely is not the same as transferring risk. If you want to get wealthy, remember that the investment part of insurance is something you should never pay for. Insurance companies try to sell us "fixed annuities," "variable annuities," and "guaranteed income" products, which are supposed investment products, but with some safety features to make us feel fuzzy and warm. If you want to get wealthy, you should not buy too much insurance, and you should not mix insurance with investments.

If you follow that rule, you will end up wealthier.

For the remainder of this chapter I'll present a few more items we should know about insurance, always keeping in mind the single question about risk transfer. These items include:

- Definitions of common insurance terms.
- The special case for life insurance.
- Term vs. whole life.
- Key man life insurance.
- Estate planning.
- Lowering insurance company costs.

Definitions of Terms

Premium: The premium is how much you pay for your risk transfer. This might be an annual payment, like in some life insurance or homeowner's policies, or it might be a monthly payment. The premium makes up the cost of the insurance you've bought. When you stop paying the regular premium, the insurance company stops guaranteeing your risk. Your policy lapses.

Premiums for life insurance are supposed to be fixed, and many term and whole life policies have a fixed premium for the life of the policy.

However, some whole life insurance providers—ones that may advertise through television with well-known celebrities—adjust their premium upward after 2 or 5 years, a policy that will on the whole discourage customers from keeping their insurance over time. This seems to me like a particularly nasty trick to cause whole life policies to lapse as people age.

Incidentally, you paying a lot of life insurance premiums, and then you dropping the insurance because it gets too expensive or your needs change, so the company never pays you out, is a key business strategy of the whole life insurance business.

Deductible: This is the amount of loss out of your own pocket you will suffer before the insurance company covers the loss. With homeowner's insurance, for example, a $1,000 deductible means that with a $25,000 roof repair due to damages, you will be reimbursed $24,000 because the first $1,000 is on you. A $5,000 auto insurance claim with a $500 deductible means that you'll receive a check for $4,500 to reimburse you for automobile damage, the net amount after your deductible.

As a rule, the higher your deductible, the lower your premium. This makes business sense because the insurance company is obliged to pay out less money to a claim, so will charge less money for the insurance.

As a general wealth-building finance rule, for certain kinds of mandatory insurance policies—like auto insurance and homeowner's insurance—the best financial bet is to choose a high deductible, because it will lower your premium.

Your ability to choose a high deductible, in turn, depends on your financial strength to endure a loss.

If you have, say, at least $5,000 in savings in the bank, you can afford to choose the $1,000 deductible for an automobile accident. If the rare accident happens and you need to pay the first $1,000 for repairs, you won't be wiped out getting your car fixed. By contrast, if you have little savings or you run a credit card balance every month, you probably need to choose the $100 deductible. Your insurance will cost more, but you've got to do what you've got to do.

Over a lifetime you will pay far more for auto insurance if you choose the low deductible. So, high deductible insurance policies are an example of the "the rich get richer," because with lots of money in the bank you can afford to have low-cost insurance and save the premium money. This principle applies to renter's or homeowner's insurance as well. Choosing the high deductible will likely save you money in the long run, as long as you can afford it.

This principle of choosing the high deductible follows from the number one risk transfer rule of insurance: if you can afford the loss, then you don't need to transfer the risk. Just keep the risk of loss, which you can afford, and save your money.

Coverage: Insurance policies generally have a maximum coverage amount, which is basically the highest amount the insurance company could possibly pay out when the unlikely bad event happens. In the case of auto insurance, the coverage for loss of the automobile will probably resemble the replacement cost of the vehicle, maybe in the tens of thousands. Similarly, for homeowner's insurance, your coverage amount will be around the cost of replacing your home, which might run hundreds of thousands up to millions (should you be so fortunate).

For personal liability insurance, such as the unlikely event that you hit somebody with your car, the coverage could be in the hundreds of thousands to millions, and should relate in some way to your net worth. The more money you have, the more you could owe, if found negligent.

The main thing to think about on coverage is matching it to the financial risk.

What I mean by that is this: try to avoid paying too much for overly generous coverage. Insurance is too darned expensive to buy more than you need. It's not clever, for example, to pay for $500,000 in homeowner's insurance if your house and household stuff are really only worth $300,000. Could you lower your insurance costs by updating the insurance company on the (lower) cost of your car or home? If that allows them to shrink the coverage, then maybe.

Exceptions and exclusions: Have you ever read an entire insurance policy? Me neither. Do you really know all the exclusions or exceptions in there? Mmm, well, me neither. Insurance companies always specify, in the fine print, which unfortunate events trigger their payout and which don't. I know there are many exceptions and exclusions in the insurance I purchase, but I frankly don't have a full grasp of them. As a result, it is difficult for me to advocate—from a hypocritical place—that you study this deeply. But you can know that there will be exceptions and exclusions, and that you should ask the person selling the insurance to tell you what they are, in plain language.

If the exceptions and exclusions of your policy don't fit your expectations, you may have to pay extra to get certain events included. Or you may have to seek out a secondary policy to get all your risks covered.

The Special Case of Life Insurance

On life insurance in particular I hold these truths to be self-evident. First, don't buy too much coverage. Second, buy "term" life only, not a "whole" life policy.

Too Much Coverage?

Let's say you're 27 years old, in a committed relationship, with no kids, a dog, and a decent job. How much life insurance coverage do you need? How about . . .

None?

Your partner will take the dog. You have no kids to support. If your earnings potential ends abruptly because you got hit by a train, who exactly needs the financial security that you were supposed to provide? The answer is probably nobody. There's no particular risk to be transferred. Of course, your situation could be special, but I don't generally think you should feel—as a 20-something—that your sister or parents or unmarried partner or roommate deserves a financial windfall upon your death. That's not your responsibility.

OK, fast-forward 10 years. You are married at 37, have two kids aged 4 and 7, a healthy spouse working part-time, an elderly dog, a mortgage (with 27 years of payments remaining), and a decent job. The way I figure it, the main financial risks of your death include the kids' needs through college and the mortgage. Unless you suffer from very high lifestyle costs, you don't need a $5 million life insurance policy. I think you need less than $1 million, maybe far less.

The right approach, I think, is to secure enough temporary financial relief to cover your spouse and kids while they adjust to life without you. If your spouse moves to full-time work in the event of your death, that's probably OK. If your kids readjust their expectations from private college to state school, that's probably OK, too.

Look, most people don't die around age 37. Your financial focus should be building savings and investments that will help your entire family regardless of whether you live or die. All the money you spend monthly on life insurance premiums will—hopefully—be wasted.

You should not be paying to provide a windfall in the event of your death. Rather, you should pay a minimum amount for a partial safety net as a risk transfer—plus a rock-solid savings and investment plan for life—as you plan on living for a long time. Be optimistic here.

Let's fast-forward again, to age 47. The dog has gone to his final resting place, your teenage kids are winning spelling bees and designing underwater drones at the science fair, while your spouse now works full-time, and you still have your decent job. Your mortgage still has 17 years to go. The way I see it, you have precisely 8 more years of life insurance risk to purchase. I say 8 years because that's when your youngest graduates from college at age 22. That's it. You need less than a million dollars of coverage.

Again, you're not looking to set up your spouse and kids in luxury when you tragically choke on that jalapeño poppers appetizer. You're looking to transfer the catastrophic loss-risk of your lost income, so that your family has time to recover. Yes, you still have significant mortgage debt. But after owning your house for 13 years, your family could decide to downsize the house without taking a loss on the sale. That's not a financial catastrophe. Your smarty-pants kids do need some financial security to plan on attending college. But adjusting downward the cost of college is also not a financial catastrophe. It's a manageable risk. Insurance is best when bought for the unmanageable risks.

Time flies, and you're 57. The kids don't live at home, two kittens have replaced them, and you have a small, 7-year mortgage left on your house. Your loving spouse is back to part-time work, and you enjoy your decent job. How much life insurance do you need now? At this point, would you believe . . .

None?

I mean, the kittens can return to the shelter from which they came. Your 24-year-old isn't your responsibility anymore. Seven years left on your mortgage means that the majority of your house is paid for, and the monthly payment no longer consumes so much of your monthly costs. Ideally, you have appreciable retirement funds and maybe other assets so that your spouse will not be left penniless when you collapse at the CrossFit gym from excessive double-unders and burpees. Your spouse—if the same age as you—can begin collecting Social Security as early as 5 years from now.

Remember, insurance is a risk transfer. If you have some measure of wealth by age 57, the fact that you can't earn income anymore isn't a big risk for your spouse. If your family is relatively prosperous by the time you've turned 57, you've self-insured! Your death is terribly sad. Your death is untimely. But if you're somewhat wealthy, it's not a financial risk that needs to be transferred through life insurance.

Look, I understand I've described a somewhat idealized situation. Divorces happen and they are expensive. Adult children have a habit of becoming dependents. You bought a second home—with a big 30-year mortgage—because you are an idiot and a glutton for punishment. Your car isn't paid off yet. You lost your job so the savings went away, and now you're 57 and broke again. I get it, maybe nothing I described in my timeline worked out the way you wanted it to. But guess what? Those are unfortunate developments, but they are not really solved through life insurance. In fact those are all unfortunate developments better addressed by investing decades of your surplus money (all those insurance premiums that went unspent!) to build a real investment nest egg through the magic of compound interest, as more fully described in Chapters 4, 7, 9, 13, 14, and 15.

Resist the temptation to purchase insurance as a wealth-building tool for after you die. Insurance is one of the worst ways to try to build wealth.

This is all a long-winded way of repeating the lesson: in order to get wealthy, don't buy too much insurance.

Term, Not Whole, Life

The second piece of advice—specific to life insurance—flows from the first: buy "term" life, not "whole" life.

Term life insures your dependents for a set number of years and then goes away. I describe the time line of ages 27, 37, 47, and 57 because I think it helps illustrate the age-specific life-cycle reasons to purchase insurance as a risk transfer. Premiums for term life tend to be fixed for the term of the insurance. The younger you are, the lower the premiums. As you get older, you will pay higher premiums for term life insurance. If you have specific risks to transfer when in your twenties, thirties or forties, term life insurance can be purchased relatively cheaply. Ideally, you don't need life insurance once you're older, because you've accumulated enough savings and investments that you've self-insured through personal wealth. That will save you from spending money on unnecessary and relatively more expensive term life insurance, when you are older.

Whole life promises to pay your dependents when you die, whenever that is. For most of us, statistically speaking, this will be when we're relatively old. With whole life insurance you agree to pay an annual premium to the insurance company for the rest of your life. For high-quality whole life policies, you can lock in a fixed premium for life at the time you first purchase it. Some people (not including me) believe this means you should buy whole life insurance when you are young, to lock in that low annual premium rate.

I have a whole bunch of problems with whole life insurance.

One problem is that risk-transfer needs change over time, so we shouldn't lock in purchasing insurance for the rest of our life, without knowing what future needs might be. As we get older, our need for a risk transfer should actually lessen. Our dependents, hopefully, are no longer dependent, but rather independent, adults. Our savings and investments, hopefully, provide some financial comfort to a loved one when we die. The safety net of Social Security picks up the care for our elderly surviving spouse. Medicare kicks in, lowering the costs of health care.

I mean, if you've done it right, you don't need life insurance as a risk transfer once you're old. You've self-insured by building up savings and investments. And the great news is that you can actually use that money anytime you want. You don't have to die to, you know, be wealthy.

The next problem with whole life is that it commonly includes a provision for "accumulated value" (this is mixing the risk-transfer and investment functions—avoid!) and for "borrowing against accumulated value" (this is mixing risk-transfer, investment, and debt functions—avoid!). This violates both the original rule on insurance—risk transfer only—as well as the more general rule of this book, which is to keep things as simple as possible.

A further problem is that some low-quality whole life policies—especially ones advertised on daytime television with celebrity endorsers—charge annual premiums that may increase as you get older, on a 2-year or 5-year schedule. This encourages you to stop paying and let the whole life policy lapse.

In my description of the uses and abuses of life insurance, I haven't taken into account the estate planning or the small-business continuity-planning role of life insurance. But let's briefly discuss.

Estate Planning

Some large life insurance policies get bought by or sold to wealthy families as a tax efficient way to pass on significant wealth to heirs. By paying hefty life insurance premiums before death, for example, a family patriarch could theoretically pass on tens of millions of tax-advantaged dollars to heirs. I am not an expert in this type of life insurance. If this is available to you and your family, then clearly you can afford to find someone who is an expert in this type of life insurance. Also, if this is available to you and your family, you don't need a book (like this one) on how to *grow* your wealth. You mostly just need a book on how to *preserve* your wealth. That's a different book.

Small-Business Continuity

"Key man" life insurance covers the catastrophic loss to a business of a business owner or key business leader, without whom the business may suffer. Like estate planning, I file this exception under the category of "get expert help beyond this book." I do think you should start your own business if that fits your personality (see Chapter 21), and then you might need key man life insurance, but that's a specific scenario. Most households don't have this issue.

Lowering Your Insurance Costs

With some effort, you can usually lower what you pay for insurance, whether for your auto, your home, or otherwise.

First, of course, putting one company into competition with another company likely improves your chance of getting the best price available to you. It's probably a smart idea to check on your premium rates every few years. If you started out with a poor driving record but then manage to string together some accident-free years, chances are that a little rate competition will lower your auto insurance this year.

In addition, if you build up savings and a little bit of wealth so that you have the ability to financially self-insure against sudden losses, you should ask about your deductibles and raise them. Your premiums will drop significantly, leaving you with more money in the bank.

Assume insurance companies aren't dumb and that they won't misprice your insurance. They do, however, look to lower their own risks, which they will reward by lowering your premiums.

So, ask the provider about certain behaviors or situations that you may qualify for. You may be able to rule out or create exclusions that suit you. As an example, let's say your renter's or homeowner's insurance automatically carries a $25,000 jewelry rider, insuring you up to that amount against theft, loss, or destruction of property. If you don't have valuable jewelry at home and you don't intend to ever get any, ask them what you could save per year if that $25,000 jewelry clause were eliminated. Can you get $100 back on your premium? The insurance company is happy to reduce its risk, and you're $100 richer every year. Everybody wins. Look for this kind of thing specific to your situation.

Investing Rather Than Insurance

Finally, let's review a bit of math regarding self-insuring through investments, rather than through whole life insurance. The math of compound interest—my favorite topic—kicks in here.

One way—the way I don't advocate—to insure your loved ones is to buy $1,000,000 of whole life insurance beginning at age 30 at an estimated cost of $334 per month, or about $4,000 per year. How does that compare to just investing that amount?

Beginning at age 30 you could choose to pay $334 per month to your insurance company for the next 45 years until, let's say, age 75. All along the way, your whole life policy would pay out $1,000,000 in the event of your unfortunate death. If you do not die, however, the life insurance policy by age 75 cannot be exchanged for any value. You cannot enjoy any fruits of your consistent and prudent payments. Instead, you must continue to make payments on it, for the rest of your life, just to have your heirs eventually get that $1,000,000 death benefit. Fail to make a premium payment along the way, and the policy lapses and you'll get no benefit at all.

If you had decided to invest the $334 per month, and managed to earn a relatively realistic 6.25% annual return on those investments, your account by age 75 would be worth $1,001,121. I did that calculation in my spreadsheet by adding up a series of future values of $334 per month, at a yield of 6.25%. After studying Chapter 4 carefully, I know you could do the same math. And yes, I picked a 6.25% return because that led almost perfectly to the $1 million result, to make my math example pretty.

The advantage of this $1,000,000 investment account, obviously, is that you don't have to die to enjoy it. It's your money for the spending. If you die immediately, at age 75, you will, of course, leave the proceeds to your heirs. Just like a life insurance policy. But you don't have to. I recommend instead that you buy a Harley Davidson and just start driving in any direction you choose. Why not? It's your money, not the insurance company's money.

Even better, at any point before age 75, you could decide to make a different plan with your money. In my view, self-insuring through consistent investment beats whole life insurance every time.

What about term life insurance?

Let's say alternatively that starting at age 30 you buy a series of 10-year term life policies. At age 30 you buy 10 years of $1,000,000 of coverage, you renew that at age 40, and then again at age 50, and then you stop purchasing life insurance. This, by the way, is not a bad plan. It takes you through age 60, at which point hopefully most of your dependents have left the house and you're merely responsible for a couple of dogs and a goldfish. Your death would be sad, but not a catastrophic, financial risk. Your spouse, hopefully, can draw from retirement accounts and Social Security in the coming years.

Let's say these monthly premiums cost $21, $29, and $75 to purchase per month, at age 30, 40, and 50. Those are low, but reasonable, 10-year term life rates I took from competitive online quotes.

Let's further assume, for comparison purposes, that you don't die and your 30 years of term life premiums go "wasted." The future value of all those insurance payments, by the time you are 75, and assuming a 6.25% return, would reach $86,062. On the downside, you've "wasted" your money because you didn't die (note: that's actually an upside). But financially, forgoing just $86K is a much cheaper option than the whole life policy. That's a reasonable price to pay to transfer financial risk from you to an insurance company. Which is the whole point.

Even if you continued to purchase term life for another 15 years after age 60, at monthly premiums of $214 for 10 years and $609 for 5 more years, your accumulated value would only reach $177,854. I don't recommend that, but compare it to whole life. It still beats the cost of the 45 years of monthly whole life insurance, which costs essentially $1,000,000 for a $1,000,000 death benefit.

Some would argue that, if I'm going to buy term life insurance for 30 years, between ages 30 and 60, that I should just lock that in at age 30, because the premiums will be lower. Maybe. I might be able to get 30 years of term life for about $60, beginning at age 30.

The reason I'd personally choose instead to renew each decade is that my insurance needs may rise, or they may drop, decade upon decade. If I have a $5 million net worth at age 50, for example, I'd argue that my risk-transfer needs have disappeared. I'd no longer need to buy any life insurance. Conversely, if life became unexpectedly more expensive or I acquired many more dependents, I may need to buy more coverage in a subsequent decade. Revisiting the issue of term life every 10 years allows for flexibility and adjustment to life's needs.

Really Unnecessary Insurance

Finally, I hope that by pointing out the number one question about insurance—"What's the risk-transfer need?"—you will know how to avoid unnecessary insurance products, like whole life insurance. What else can you avoid?

Most product warranties. You buy the $500 electronics product. The salesperson wants to sell you the $35 warranty. But, what's the risk? Can you afford a $500 loss on that electronics product? Of course you can; you just spent that amount on an electronics product. I mean, you won't like to lose it. You won't be happy when the product fails. But it's not really a big financial risk for you personally. As a result, you don't need the warranty.

Optional insurance at the car rental place. Do you drive a car and have auto insurance yourself? Yes, you do, which means you have most personal liability for accidents covered. Do you have a credit card? Most often, through that, you have additional auto coverage for car rentals. As a result, you may have very little financial risk to insure. Very probably, you don't need optional auto insurance at the car rental place.

The list of unnecessary insurance goes on from there, as the insurance industry figures out additional ways to extract premiums from us based on our emotions and fears. Try to resist. Or at least, try to really test in your mind whether you have a big financial risk that you need to transfer away from yourself to an insurance company. If it's not a big risk, save your money. You will get wealthier in the long run.

CHAPTER SEVENTEEN

On Work

Your First Job

If you are applying for, or working in, your first job following graduation, I have two pieces of hard-won knowledge for you:

1. The pay for this first job is insufficient to actually, you know, live decently. (I'll explain why in a moment.)
2. This doesn't have to be, and probably isn't, your job for life. (And that's a good thing, even if you like your first job.)

The Pay

About the pay: What new graduates may not realize is that wherever you live—whether a small town or a big city—the cost of living is set by and for people who make much more money than you do. In your early twenties you'll be procuring housing, paying for transportation (whether car or bus or subway or bicycle), and purchasing food in a place that is affordable for people already in their thirties, forties, fifties, and sixties. People—in other words—who already have decades of promotions, bonuses, savings, and cost-of-living adjustments behind them. Most of these folks can afford restaurants, cars, and houses that you simply cannot, on your starting salary.

If you're a recent graduate, you don't have decades of promotions and bonuses baked into your compensation. Unless you were born into a fortunate family, most likely you do not have much in savings either.

None of this setup is "fair" necessarily. But you know what? "Fair" is for kids. Age discrimination in favor of one's elders is one of the few discriminations that I can stomach. (Especially, of course, the older I get.)

My point about the pay being insufficient to actually live in your chosen town or city is simply that many things about your job may be wrong, including how little you get paid. It hurts. Every big thing you need to pay for is priced for people who make more than you. It's possibly untenable. It's also nearly universal. Probably the only way to survive financially is to adopt some of the attitudes discussed in Chapter 7 on saving money. For a while to come you'll need a crappier car and a crappier housing situation than you'd prefer. You'll eat out less. Modesty of needs, in these first few years, is probably the only way to keep from falling behind financially.

One saving grace of the first job, however, is that hopefully soon you can move up in pay, or move up in quality of work, or both.

Later Jobs

Maybe you'll be so lucky as to find both a good paying job and your "life's calling" right away. But probably you won't, or probably you didn't. What you do next—at job 2—is hopefully a closer approximation to what you should actually work at for a living.

I know it seems like a lot to ask to actually seek out work that is your "calling," since getting from today to the next paycheck may be the most heroic financial accomplishment available to you at this point. I get that. But we're momentarily in the fantasy realm, not the reality realm.

Speaking of the fantasy realm, a good way to know if you're in the right kind of work is to take the "lottery test."

Lottery Test

I think everyone should periodically—let's say once a year—run the lottery test in their own head. The lottery test, as maybe you've guessed, is the thought experiment of "If I won the lottery—such that I wouldn't have to work at my current job anymore—would I quit doing what I'm doing for work?"

Conversely, if you would choose to continue to work at your same job, even after the pay became irrelevant, then you "pass" the lottery test. Cleary, if you would stay in that job without needing the money, you've found your calling.

For a long time—and I suspect this is true for a majority of people—I failed the lottery test, in the sense that I would have happily given up my job if I had won the lottery.

Here's my strongly held belief: if you fail the lottery test, you need to keep looking for better work. Not necessarily more highly paid work, or more prestigious work, but rather better work for you, your skills, your belief systems, and your talents.

About the lottery, I want to share a true story and true confession. Around the time I was writing this chapter, the national Powerball jackpot rolled over enough to hit a level that a gambler who plays the "odds" could justifiably, sort of, purchase a ticket.

So I played the lottery.

Let me be clear. Playing the lottery is a terrible, terrible idea that I cannot justify in the least. In this hypocritical case of me buying a Powerball ticket, do as I say, not as I do. Recall from Chapter 7 on savings that gambling will only hurt you in the long run. Don't do this.

But one good thing did result from my wasted gamble:

I felt a sense of panic, not about losing $2, but rather the opposite. I started thinking, "What if I win?"

I would *have* to stop doing what I love, which is helping people think more clearly about their personal finance choices. *Because nobody, obviously, would ever take seriously the personal finance advice of a guy who played, and won, the lottery.*

First, because playing the lottery is a fool's activity, my credibility would be completely shot. I could light my money on fire and toss it out the window while driving 90 miles an hour down the highway and build more credibility than I would by playing and winning the lottery.

Second, who would ever take my advice seriously, when the retort to every serious thing I say would be "OK, easy for you to say Mr-Save-Your-Money-and-Invest-in-an-IRA-While-Still-in-Your-Twenties. You yourself got rich by playing the lottery."

LOTTERY AND POKER ODDS

The odds of winning that particular lottery I participated in were listed as 1 in 292 million, with a promised immediate lump sum payout of around $900 million. Theoretically, if the immediate payout of the lottery is higher than 292 million to 1, a gambler could—conceivably—argue that there's "positive expected value" in a lottery. What I mean is that, if you pay $2 for a ticket, and if the net payout is bigger than $584 million ($2 \times 292$ million, but you knew that) you've got a large enough payout to justify the gamble. You have "pot-odds," in poker-speak, and "correct" poker play is built on this principle. In this particular case, after taxes and taking into account the probability of multiple winners splitting the pot, even the superior pot-odds don't justify the gamble, because you won't ever win. In reality, a lifetime of playing even "positive expected value" pot-odds with lottery tickets will leave you much poorer than if you simply saved (or better yet—invested) your money. So, like I said, never play the lottery.

I literally felt *agita* at the thought of having to give up everything I enjoy about being a finance guide, if I had won the Powerball.

Which, when you think about, is a pretty good sign. I'm probably working at the right thing. No, I know I'm working at the right thing. Writing this book has been a true joy for me. It ain't for the money, believe me.

Some Writers' Views on Their Work

Speaking of writing for a living, I recently met with an elderly friend-of-a-friend who had published numerous well-received history books and who regularly appeared in the *The New York Review of Books*. On the subject of retirement as he got older, he said to me rhetorically, "How could I retire? I mean, who would I even tell? This is what I do. I write." He painted a picture of a man ready to keep on writing until the words simply stopped coming. I could tell right then he chose the right kind of work for his talents and interests.

I don't recommend writing as a good financial choice for anyone, but I'm also reminded of the late David Foster Wallace, a troubled writer who nevertheless exuded joy in his craft. He wrote in a letter to his friend, the novelist Jonathan Franzen:

"I think back with much saliva to the times in 1984, 85, 86, 87 when I'd sit down and look up and it would be hours later and there'd be this mess of filled up notebook paper and I just felt wrung out and well fucked and well blessed."[1]

Are you working at a job that gives you that same feeling, working so many hours that pass like minutes?

How Does This Build Wealth?

What does this have to do with getting wealthy over the long run? Just this.

If you take an aptitude test for which career you should seek—whether it be the Myers-Briggs test, the Johnson O'Connor aptitude test, the Strengths Finder test, or the multistep work in *What Color Is Your Parachute*—the lessons are always the same: try to match up your innate skills and interests with your paid profession. (By the way, I've taken all of these. I love tests.)

That way, work doesn't feel so much like a way to pay your rent. It feels instead like a calling. It feels instead like an expression of who you are in the world. It feels instead like a game that you are uniquely suited to play

---

[1]As quoted by D. T. Max, "The Unfinished," *New Yorker*, March 9, 2009.

in the world. It feels instead like a thing from which you would never retire. It would feel like: "this is who I am, this is what I do."

One of my bond salesman mentors at Goldman once told me that, for him, selling bonds was a lot like playing professional baseball. He reacted to the balls hit into the field with sure-footed moves. I noticed that he always seemed to know just what to say to both clients and colleagues. He performed one of the world's most stressful jobs with a mischievous grin on his face and an instinct for creating great solutions to everyone's problems.

I never was able to sell bonds like him. Frankly, the job wasn't a great fit for my skills, talents, and beliefs. Many days I'd go home from work with a headache, made simultaneously anxious and bored by the day's grind. For me, this felt like a well-paid but crushing way to spend my waking hours. For my mentor, by contrast, this was a thrilling game to play each day.

In a related story, I left after 6 years and he made partner quickly. In the course of my writing this book he got promoted to one of the top positions at the firm. I won't be in the least surprised if he runs the firm some day. He found a job that matched his particular skills. I often think of his professional baseball metaphor. At this point he's certainly being paid like a Hall of Fame–bound major league ball player.

19th-Century Cultural Attitudes on Work

In the United States we traditionally celebrate individuals who get wealthy through hard work, invention, and business building. Today, think Bill Gates and Mark Zuckerberg. Heroes like them from earlier centuries include Eli Whitney, Thomas Edison, and Henry Ford.

The national cultural myth of their wealthy heroism depends primarily on the idea that they worked hard. They did not sit idle. One shorthand in the United States for this idea is the Horatio Alger myth of boot-strapping oneself up from poverty to wealth, through work.

In the United Kingdom—the country besides Canada with whom we share the most cultural affinity—work traditionally has carried a very different meaning. The national myth of England from the 19th century contrasts sharply from the Horatio Alger myth. The English novels of Jane Austen and Anthony Trollope depict an elite whose wealth derives entirely from inherited property.

Simply put, they never work. Rather, they seek suitable marriages of both romance and financial convenience to continue their idle lives as nonworking gentlemen and gentlewomen. The worst nightmare of Austen and Trollope protagonists would be the reduction of their wealth to the point where they would be forced to actually, you know, work for a living. And they fear that work with good reason. We have an idea from their near contemporary, the novelist Charles Dickens, of the condition of workers in *Hard Times* and *Oliver Twist*. Only the most unfortunates of society would seek a working-man's life.

While I acknowledge the appeal of the fantasy of 19th-century English gentlemen—and partly I read Austen and Trollope to live in that fantasy—I prefer the American myth about work.

We grow up with the cultural assumption in the United States that work can build wealth in our lifetime. We also believe work confers status, meaning, and quite possibly, heroism.

I'm not saying people universally love their work in the United States. To be sure, many to most of us would rather not be doing what we're doing to earn money. "Take this job and shove it!" seems as close to an American anthem as any other great classic country song.

I'm just saying that work at its best confers honor, meaning, and attachment to the world.

If you leave work like I did in bond sales with a headache each day—simultaneously bored and anxious—that's probably a sign you should keep looking for a better fit.

If instead you find work that binds you to yourself, and to others, you have a chance at this. If you can find work that leaves you feeling "well fucked and well blessed" at the end of the day, then you have a chance at this.

If we had that feeling, we would no doubt choose to work as long as we could. What would be the point of retiring? We would do this regardless of the pay. This is who we are. This is what we do. That's a very optimistic thought.

Work as a Prerequisite for Wealth

When I say that work is necessary to be wealthy, I mean that in at least two senses.

The first most obvious way is that getting paid at work helps us in turn pay for daily necessities, repay our debts, build a monthly surplus, and supply the money for long-term investing. If we're particularly well suited to our work, we will likely excel at it and advance in our careers like my Goldman mentor, ascending the professional ladder nimbly, with a mischievous smile on our faces.

The second less obvious way is what I've been saying when I talk about the lottery test, David Foster Wallace, and my preference for the Horatio Alger myth over a Trollope novel, at least for our real, 21st-century life.

A majority of us are not "wealthy"—in the truest sense of the word—in part because we haven't found work we would keep doing even if we won the lottery. We haven't, in other words, found work that we would do in complete disregard for whether it pays the bills or not. Work that we do regardless of pay is a hallmark of truly wealthy people. (Hold that thought, if you don't mind, until the Epilogue of Chapter 21, in which we finally talk about what "wealthy" really means.)

If you find yourself waiting impatiently until the end of the day, or the end of the week, or until retirement, anticipating the moment when you can stop doing what you're doing, then you are far from that place. That's OK, just keep looking for better work. That attitude toward work is a signal that you need to make a new plan. You're not getting truly wealthy this way.

Maybe that is just the signal you need to start a job search. Or maybe you're unhappy enough to become an entrepreneur. Entrepreneurship happens to correlate with happiness at work, as well as wealth creation. But that's the subject of Chapter 21.

PART 5

Feeling Wealthier

CHAPTER EIGHTEEN

On Retirement

The Golden Years?

The biggest mistake we make about retirement is the idea that we'll finally get to do all the fun or important stuff, once we stop working. My ham radio passion will finally blossom. Look out competitive orchid conventions, because here I come! Travel to all the island countries of the world will now commence!

I guess, maybe, but I'm skeptical.

I already mentioned in Chapter 17 my favorite view on retirement from a successful writer who once told me "How could I retire? I mean, who would I even tell? This is what I do. I write." Although admittedly as a writer he enjoyed independence from any particular "boss" or a company, his attitude toward work and retirement strikes me as the right one, an attitude to which we should all aspire. If you've found a vocation that suits your talents and interests, then retirement isn't something you seek. It's not something you could even do, and still be you. If you like what you do, and you're good it, retirement should be simply a slowing down of your vocation. You should ideally seek out less of the grind and more of the parts that you really like.

In retirement, ideally, you keep doing what you're doing, at the pace you prefer. If that's what you seek in retirement, you can be pretty sure you're in the right line of work. If you're counting the days until that gold watch, by contrast, you might not be in the right line of work.

If you've invested properly, then retirement choices can be made without regard to the profitability of work.

Asset Allocation Changes

Speaking of investments, what should change in retirement?

I periodically get asked questions from retirees about whether they should shift investments in their portfolio, now that they are retired. I assume that 95% of investment advisers would say yes. Indeed conventional wisdom says that you'll want more predictability and safety in retirement, so more bonds and fewer stocks, for example.

Or they'll advocate some classic numerical formula like "subtract your age from 120, and that's the percent of your portfolio that should remain in stocks. The rest in bonds."

Simple rules are nice, but here, again, I'm skeptical.

If you retire with decades of your life ahead of you, a better answer may be to keep the pedal to the stock market metal. Remember the arguments in Chapters 13 and 14 about the proper mix of risky and nonrisky assets, otherwise known as stocks and bonds? The longer you have to live, the more overwhelmingly clear the odds are that risky assets—stocks—will outperform even over your remaining life.

You might live 30 more years after you retire. I can say with high confidence that a diversified portfolio of stocks will far outperform any bonds you could own for 30 years. Even if you only live 10 more years after retirement, the odds still favor stocks over bonds by a heavy margin.

A blend with bonds will cushion any volatility, true, but as we've seen, that volatility is just on paper only. Remain optimistic. You are not going to sell when the market is down. Therefore, who cares if the stock market bumps up and down in price. Keep your eye on the longest time horizon.

Required Minimum Distributions

Having said all that, I'll introduce a modest correction to my hard-core attitude toward stocks and bonds. In the United States, tax-advantaged retirement accounts such as 401(k), 403(b), and traditional IRAs all have a required minimum distribution (RMD) per year after a certain age, currently 70.5 years.

That rule forces you, the retirement account owner, to take money out of your account. For the government's purposes, you must pay income tax on that distributed money that year. The amount of money you must take out depends on how much "remaining life" you (or your spouse) have, according to an official actuarial table kept by the IRS.[1]

---

[1]Note that the RMD rules apply to a traditional IRA, but not a Roth IRA. Retirees with a Roth IRA can choose to withdraw money at any time or any pace in retirement, or never, should they choose. The tax reason for this is that contributions to a Roth IRA were already taxed on the way in the

If the IRS actuarial table says you have 17 years of your life left at age 70, then the RMD formula says you must withdraw the value of your account divided by 17. With a $1 million retirement account at age 70 that would work out to $58,824, because $1 million divided by 17 is $58,824. With a $1 million retirement account at age 80, with a remaining life expectancy of 10 years, for example, the RMD would be $100,000, because $1 million divided by 10 is $100,000.

The reason why I'd moderate my views on the proper stock and bond mix late in life is that the federal government—through the RMD—forces a sale and distribution of cash out of your retirement account. If you knew the $100,000 of a $1 million stock portfolio had to be liquidated this year, and a similar amount for the next few years, then it might make sense to keep some amount in nonrisky assets. It would feel sad to have the market drop 35% just before having to liquidate one-seventeenth, or one-tenth, of a retirement account.

So, should you keep, say, 30% of a retirement account portfolio in non-risky assets for easy liquidation? I'm not going to do it personally. The odds still favor an all-risky portfolio. But it's not crazy either.

Of course, with any investment portfolio held outside of a retirement account like a 401(k), 403(b), or IRA, you do not have to comply with RMD requirements. You can time your withdrawals as you see fit, without the government demanding you make withdrawals according to their estimated-remaining-life tables. If the market crashes, and assuming you don't need the money right away, then if you don't want to withdraw money from your non-retirement account, you don't have to.

There's an argument in there somewhere for building a fully taxable, or nonretirement account portfolio, in addition to your retirement portfolio.

---

account, and thereby entitle the retiree to tax-free distributions. Recall that traditional IRAs receive a tax-break upon contribution, but will be taxed as ordinary income upon distribution. Both are great tax-advantaged accounts with one benefiting you on the way in, and the other benefiting you on the way out.

CHAPTER NINETEEN

On Estate Planning

My first rule of estate planning goes against the grain of our culture: you don't need to leave any money to your heirs.

I say this because, generally speaking, children don't deserve free money. They're apt to blow it all on unnecessary downloads and overpriced lattes. Especially the way you raised them, those ungrateful punks. I'm sort of kidding about the punks part, but not the rule itself. Your concern in growing wealthy should be your own needs first. The most important legacy to leave your children is a strong character and set of values, experiences, plus unconditional love. That's a legacy better than a pile of money in the bank.

My second rule of estate planning is that of course you should hire an attorney to professionally prepare a will, a power of attorney document, and a health proxy document. Why should you hire an attorney instead of downloading a cheaper version from the interwebs? For the same reason you should hire somebody else to do your taxes each year: you are apt to save money and avoid costly mistakes by hiring an expert who knows the specific rules that apply to your geography and financial situation.

My third rule of estate planning is: do it NOW.

When is a good time to prepare your first will? Now. Create a will as soon as you live on your own, not as a dependent. You might not have any real appreciable assets yet, but be optimistic. Remember the power of compound interest, the most powerful force in the universe. Steady accumulation, combined with an unwavering faith in risky assets, may create a large snowball of assets some day. You don't owe the people who outlive you your money, but you do owe them clarity and simplicity. So save them the hassle and get it legally sorted. Again: Now.

The Main Principles

So now that you know that you don't need to leave money to heirs but you do need to create a will and end-of-life documents as soon as possible, what is there left to say?

Not much, except two important principles, and two specific life hacks, that follow naturally from those principles.

The first principle is KISS—keep it simple stupid. This should seem obvious at this point in the book, since it's the same idea said many places and in many ways. Remember: Simple beats complicated almost every time. Low cost beats high cost. Avoid complexity. Be very skeptical if you're doing something complex, just for the taxes.

For example, many wealthy people—more than you would expect unless you come from or live in that world—decide where to live throughout the year based on where income tax and estate taxes are the lowest. They and their accountants expend extraordinary effort to make sure not more than half of their days in any year (for example) are lived in a particular high-tax state. At the upper reaches of wealth and income of course this kind of attention to detail can be worth tens of millions of dollars, so naturally it's the sort of thing accountants and lawyers suggest. But when you really think about it—if you have that kind of wealth, shouldn't you be able to do and go and be whatever you damn well please? At a certain point, if you're making major life choices (like where to spend your summers or winters and which neighbors and friends to spend them with) based on the taxes—I don't know what to tell you except that you're doing it wrong. That's one example of what I mean about letting the taxes tail wag the life dog.

Similarly, complicated estate tax planning strategies—especially at the upper end of the wealth scale—may require you to go through elaborate schemes to pass on wealth with the minimal tax hit. These are all clever and great except that I'd urge deep skepticism about whether the cleverness—and the cost of the cleverness—are really worth it in the end. Should you be fortunate enough to qualify for high-end estate planning techniques, just remember the main lessons about simplicity, low cost, and not letting taxes dictate important life choices. So, again, KISS.

The second principle any good estate planner will tell you is that the heart of any plan must be your personal values. The key estate-planning question shouldn't be about how to move the largest chunk of money to the next generation and philanthropies, but rather: What do I believe in? What do I stand for? What was it all for?

If you can make your personal values the center of your estate plan, then you've gone a long way toward a good plan.

Two Estate-Planning Life Hacks

Most of us will not need high-end estate-planning techniques, so I'll just offer the two following estate-planning hacks that are super-duper simple and can help people of relatively modest estates. Eventually (of course, as a result of reading this book) you will have so much money and assets that you'll be tempted to engage in complicated and expensive estate planning (resist that temptation!), but until then, you can feel clever with these two cheap and easy-to-manage ideas:

1. The magical Roth IRA
2. Donor-advised funds

Let's take these one at a time.

Estate Planning Life Hack 1: The Magical Roth IRA

As much as I kind of hate the idea of estate planning, I do get excited by the super-cheap, modest, intergenerational tax-free wealth transfer available through the Roth IRA.

The mechanics of a Roth IRA may change in the future, but as of now the Roth offers you—under specific circumstances—an unusually simple and cheap intergenerational wealth-transfer tool. It's a life hack just for an older you, in your wealthy retirement.

Here are the three key ingredients to the magical Roth IRA life hack, which I'll describe in more detail below the list.

1. You don't withdraw from the Roth IRA, because you don't have to.
2. Income from the Roth IRA is tax-free, forever.
3. Choose a very young heir for your Roth IRA, and he or she can enjoy increasing tax-free income that increases throughout his or her lifetime.

Don't Withdraw

Roth IRAs differ from a traditional IRA in that retirees are not required to take minimum distributions each year. Simply stated, if you had $100,000 in a traditional IRA and $100,000 in a Roth IRA, the IRS rules would require you to take out money from the traditional, but not the Roth, each year.

As mentioned in the last chapter, the amount you take out in required minimum distribution (RMD) is determined by an IRS table that tells you, at every age, what your expected remaining years of life are—and based on that, how much of your traditional retirement account you must withdraw that year.

To take a simplified example, an 80-year-old man might have 10 years of "expected remaining life," according to the IRS table, and therefore must withdraw at least one-tenth of his traditional retirement account. An 89-year-old may have 6 years of "expected remaining life" according to the IRS table and therefore must withdraw at least one-sixth of his traditional retirement account.

To repeat from above, the Roth IRA has no RMD, so a relatively wealthy person could die with a larger Roth IRA than a traditional IRA because of smaller, or zero, withdrawals in retirement years. If you have enough to live on in retirement without withdrawing from your Roth, then you'll end up with a bigger amount to pass on to heirs. I mention all this in some detail because it forms step one of the magical Roth IRA life hack.

Tax-Free Income

Step two is that, as stated in Chapter 18, all income from Roth IRA distributions may be enjoyed tax-free. So any heir who withdraws money from a Roth account will pay no taxes on that income, ever. Depending on income tax rates, that makes the money between 20% and 40% bigger than it would otherwise be. Which is pretty sweet.

THE MAGICAL ROTH IRA: APPLYING COMPOUND INTEREST MATH

Using simple compound interest math from Chapter 4 we can see the long-term tax-free income potential of the inherited magical Roth IRA life hack.

Let's say the fortunate great-grandchild inherited a $100,000 Roth IRA at age 12, and let's further suppose the great-grandchild intends to only take the required minimum distribution for life, in order to maximize lifetime tax-free income. I'm going to further assume a 70-year life expectancy for the 12-year-old in the first year of inheritance. Finally, let's assume the account earns 6% per year for the great-grandchild's lifetime. How big does the account grow, and how much will the heir receive per year?

Under these assumptions, the account will grow from $100,000 at age 12 to approximately $578,000 by age 65. Annual distributions of tax-free income will grow from $1,400 in the first year to $34,000 by age 65. The total amount of tax-free income distributed between age 12 and age 65 will total approximately $557,000. Not a bad result from an initial $100,000 Roth IRA inheritance.

Young Heirs

Step three takes advantage of the fact that you can designate the heir—or beneficiary—of your Roth IRA to be whomever you want. You as the original retiree could choose to forgo distributions from a Roth. However, your designated beneficiary must begin annual withdrawals, initially subject to an IRS life-expectancy table, when it comes to annual required minimum distributions.

Well, what's the big deal there, you may skeptically ask? The big deal is that if you designate grandchildren or even great-grandchildren as heirs, then the life expectancy table allows that heir to take out only a small percentage of the account value each year from the Roth IRA. A 33-year-old heir, for example, might have 50 years of remaining life, so could choose to only withdraw one-fiftieth (or 2%) of the account value as income in the first year following inheritance. Even better, a 12-year-old heir might have 70 years of expected life remaining, so would withdraw only one-seventieth (or 1.4%) in the first year following inheritance.

The "remaining expected life" for the heir then reduces by one for every year thereafter. Our theoretical 12-year-old must withdraw one-seventieth in the first year, then one-sixty-ninth in the second year, one-sixty-eighth in the third year, and so on.

So why is that a good thing as a wealth transfer? That's good because, invested properly (see again, Chapters 13 and 14) the inherited Roth IRA probably continues to grow throughout the lifetime of the heir, to become significantly larger than it was when first inherited, generating an increasing amount of tax-free income for the heir. If you only take out 1.4% or 2% of the account value each year, it should be possible for an heir to enjoy an increasing legacy of tax-free income. That's the life hack.

Alternatively, you may feel free to ignore all of this semi-complicated life hack for the simple principle stated above, that children—and especially grandchildren—do not deserve free money. It's up to you.

Estate Planning Life Hack 2: Donor-Advised Funds

Brokerage firms that advise wealthy families report two big problems in estate planning. First, many families decide to pass on assets to heirs and charities only *after* they die. Second, a majority of wealthy families worry about the negative effects of passing on money to heirs.

Traditionally, a wealthy family with philanthropic intentions could set up a charitable foundation, reaping tax benefits while at the same time doing good work in the world. The costs of setup and maintenance of foundations, however, traditionally make them sensible above, say, $25 million. That's a lovely solution for certain families but isn't so practical or relevant for 99% of us.

And that's why donor-advised funds (DAFs) offer a super-cheap, practical, life hack.

DAFs address the problems in a low-cost, simple way at a scale that works for the rest of us. I'll explain how DAFs are the solution to many estate-planning problems, one at a time.

The problem of passing on money to heirs and charities *after* you die, rather than *before*, is multifold. First, it's more tax efficient to pass on money before your death. I know, I know, in Chapter 10 I talked about how unimportant taxes were. I don't mean to disregard taxes completely. I just mean don't do something simply to save on taxes. The second, and more important, reason to pass on money and assets before *you* pass on is that you can better express your values with your money while you're still alive.

What do I mean by that? I mean, when you give money to a charity while you are alive, you get to participate in the mission of the charity. Becoming a donor while you're still alive means you can watch the organization make use of your funds. Is it accomplishing the goal? Is it a good steward of your funds? Are there equally good or better ways to accomplish the philanthropic mission you care about most?

Giving money while you're alive also lets you be thanked by the organizations you've helped. Philanthropic groups would rather thank you personally than pay homage to a tombstone.

Just as importantly, if you're interested in passing on your values to your children, the DAF lets you select other trustees to join you in the giving process. Trustees, such as, your kids. Joining your children as fellow trustees in turn provides the platform, I believe, for addressing the key estate-planning questions: "What do we believe in? What do we stand for? What was it all for?"

So let's talk about the mechanics of a donor-advised fund. Plenty of large brokerages offer DAFs, at reasonable cost, no hassle, and low-minimum account sizes.

The ones I looked at from a few well-known brokerages charged 0.6% management fees, which seems reasonable to me, and when combined with an index mutual fund fee keeps money management costs below 1% of assets. A few required $5,000 to open an account, while another one had a $25,000 minimum, but in either case these are within reasonable range of middle-class donors rather than the multi-million-dollar fortunes generally needed to open up a charitable foundation. The average DAF account was a little less than $300,000 in recent years, but clearly we can open up and maintain these accounts for a lot less than the average.

When you find a charity you want to give to, you contact the brokerage with your instructions, they verify the legitimacy of the charity, and release funds within a day or two.

When you contribute to a DAF you:

1. Qualify for income tax relief for charitable giving, in the year of the donation.
2. Can grow your assets within the fund, tax-free, over time.
3. Can take your time choosing where to make a gift.
4. Have the opportunity to discuss with your fellow trustees (such as your children) the benefits of giving to one charity or another.

A DAF solves a whole bunch of estate-planning problems—values, children, tax efficiency, timing, appropriate (including small) scale—all in one neat package. Check it out.

When you've set up a simple will, possibly incorporating these two life hacks—a Roth IRA and a DAF—that's when you'll know you're pretty close to being wealthy. The end of this book discusses what it means to be wealthy, by my own definition. See if you agree.

PART 6

Finishing Strong: How Will You Know If You're Wealthy?

CHAPTER TWENTY

On Death

Here's a strong statement of opinion you won't see in most "personal finance" literature: I don't think you can understand the meaning of wealth—or even truly *be wealthy*—if you haven't considered your own mortality. You've got to contemplate the end.

This doesn't come naturally to most of us. I don't like thinking about it myself. If I make a mistake and think about my death right before I go to bed, well damn, I get a specific kind of age-vertigo that keeps me awake for the next 3 hours. If you're still in your twenties, the idea of death may still seem quite abstract. Death to you might be a thing—like retirement, incontinence, and arthritis—which afflicts some older people out there, but not you. If you're still in your teens and reading this, well, you just don't listen do you? I thought I told you in the first chapter to go outside and kick a soccer ball or something.

So what's the link between our death and being wealthy?

I have a few ideas.

A buddy used to joke that the best way to manage your money, with respect to death, was to spend all your money down to a zero balance so that your check to the undertaker bounces from insufficient funds at the bank. What's a check, you ask? Forget it. Also, think of the poor undertaker!

I see a couple of serious ideas in that joke, however.

First, dying penniless—as in the joke above—leaves nothing for your heirs. Is that OK? I think so.

At some fundamental level, it's completely fine. Heirs don't really need or deserve your money. Trying to figure out whether you have enough to satisfy your own cost of living as you get older is stressful enough. The additional obligation we might feel to provide for heirs seems unnecessary. If there's money left over, great, but don't stress about it.

Of course, a spouse who can't work is different, as would be a child who cannot take care of himself or herself after you've passed. Chapter 16's discussion of term insurance—to cover that risk—should take care of most situations. I acknowledge some families' situations would require you to worry about taking care of your heirs. But those should be the exceptions, and I don't think we should act like most of our family members need our money after we've died.

More fundamentally, however, I like that joke because it makes an important point. You only need money to cover your lifestyle costs until the day you die. After that, you're home free! Nobody can charge you for anything anymore. You can't and won't take it with you. The score doesn't matter anymore. You only need it to last until the final day. And if you bounce that last check— heck, it's not your problem anymore!

Remaining Life Span

When you think about it that way, you can see why the amount of money we need—our ultimate measure of personal wealth—depends on our remaining life span.

If you had one more day to live, how much money do you need? Maybe, none? At least, not much. I mean, there's a limit to how many expensive double-fudge ice cream sundaes with extra Heath Bar on top I could possibly put away on my last day on earth. Knowing me, I personally would try to push that limit. Still, there is a limit to how much I could possibly spend with just 1 day to go.

Remaining a bit longer with my imaginary scenario of just 1 more day to live, I certainly don't ever have to a work another day in my life. I probably don't need to go in to the office. Or, I'd only go in to work if I wanted to do it for some reason other than the pay.

That means my time is my own, to spend as I like. Shouldn't that sort of be one of the definitions of being wealthy? What else do we need, except the freedom to spend our days as we choose?

Now, what if you could extend that time period from 1 day to a week? Or a year? Isn't it equally true that if you have this short amount of time to live, and your lifestyle costs were covered, then you're a wealthy person? It is worth trying to build enough financial cushion to buy back your own time, time you can spend doing only exactly what you choose.

The shorter your remaining time to live—by this thought process—the less money you need to have, to completely buy back your own time. If you don't need money to live, you don't need to work for money.

This is what I mean by saying that *being wealthy* has something to do with being aware of our mortality.

Aspirational Wealth

Ideally of course, we reach that "never have to work a day in our life again" stage before our last day on earth. Ideally, we have many years of retirement, in which we work at whatever we like, but we don't need to actually make any more money.

If we can manage to build and maintain a monthly surplus (Chapter 7), stick to low-interest rate debt only (Chapter 8), start retirement investing early (Chapter 9), buy only as much car as necessary (Chapter 11), own our primary residence for a long period of time (Chapter 12), invest in higher-risk assets in a simple and low-cost way and never sell (Chapters 13 and 14), buy only as much insurance as necessary (Chapter 16), and find work that we actually enjoy (Chapter 17), then a wealthy retirement becomes as inevitable as the sun rising in the east every morning.

And if we are fortunate enough to build our own successful business (Chapter 21), we might just blow up the ceiling on our monetary wealth. Entrepreneurial wealth—compared to wealth derived from working for someone else—offers a much greater possibility of that intergenerational wealth.

Whatever monetary wealth we accumulate, however, that amount will no doubt pale in comparison to the value of nonmonetary things, as we ponder our mortality.

Atul Gawande

Physician Atul Gawande is one of our best thinkers on death and what it means to live a good life even as our health deteriorates. A main lesson of his meditation on dying well, *Being Mortal,* is that extra end-of-life medical expenditures do not necessarily help us. Our ability to order additional procedures and interventions at the end of our life may in fact get in the way of us thinking about what our real priorities are, with our remaining time. If presented with the choice, do I really prefer 6 more months of life—wracked by pain and horrific medicines—or would a few weeks of relative comfort surrounded by my closest friends and family serve me better? More is not necessarily better when it comes to medical treatment. Less medicine, or at least a thoughtful discussion about priorities and trade-offs, could help most of us die better.

Returning to the subject of death and wealth, the "less is better" theme makes sense to me. I think somewhere in those modest thoughts is a key to "being wealthy."

I mean, naturally, we know end-of-life medical care drives families into bankruptcy. We may throw tens of thousands of dollars as families, and hundreds of thousands of dollars as a society, at keeping a body alive, possibly well after a high quality of life is long gone. And that is a tough financial choice many, or all of us, have faced or will face. But that isn't exactly what I'm most concerned with, with respect to the idea of modesty and "less is better."

Rather, I suspect that if we really think about it—in the light of our inevitable mortality—the key elements that make us feel wealthy at the end of our life have little to do with money.

What is the price of a sunset holding my daughter's hand, neither of us saying anything but both understanding each other's thoughts? What would I pay for a single pain-free week, once my body betrayed me and began to hurt all over? Would I spend a king's ransom to salsa dance with my wife again, had I lost that ability? Yes, I know I would. The relative value of money—versus experiences costing almost nothing—shifts when we think about our own decline and death.

The tart first bite of an apple. Companionship. The soft cheek of an infant. A tragic joke that makes you laugh and cry until your stomach hurts. An overcast afternoon digging in the sand, building a sandcastle that won't last past high tide. If those don't make you feel infinitely wealthy, well then, I don't know what will.

Death Is Guaranteed

Here's my only 100% personal guarantee in this book. You will die.

No vitamins, hot sulfur soaks, or paleo diets prevent that. You can spend your money any way you like, but aging (if you're lucky!) and death (guaranteed!) can't be pushed off indefinitely.

All we can do is try to be—and feel—wealthy in our short interim on the planet.

I recommend staying skeptical of costly placebos which purport to offer the fountain of youth. We foolish humans have been looking for that forever. Don't hold your breath on a cure for death. Forget the crèmes and potions, pills and powders, diets and fads. Save your money. Bite the apple. Eat the hot fudge sundae. None of our sand castles survive the high tide.

CHAPTER TWENTY-ONE

Epilogue: On Being Wealthy

This Epilogue stands apart from the other chapters in this book.

I say this in part because while I believe every previous chapter has universal application and you should follow the advice contained in it entirely to the letter, I don't believe that as much about this chapter. You don't *have* to act on this advice. Some people, because of personality, risk tolerance, or a different set of beliefs, probably shouldn't act on this advice.

On the other hand, you should be aware of the most important ideas here, about entrepreneurship and philanthropy. It took me until the third and fourth decades of my life to learn all these things. If you're not there yet, maybe this chapter will save you some time. Also, I think these two ideas have a lot to do with happiness, which shouldn't be dismissed as an important goal.

Finally, in this Epilogue I deliver my long-promised definition of what being wealthy means, so you should stick around for that, just before we roll the final credits.

Entrepreneurship

Here's one main idea on entrepreneurship: the only way to get really rich is through building your own business. The wealthiest fortunes in the world are all entrepreneurial fortunes (or people who inherited fortunes from entrepreneurs). In order to build extraordinary wealth, you have to be a business owner, not a business employee.

Building your own business, of course, will be incredibly risky and stressful. The journey is unlikely to be smooth. It's not for the risk-averse. You should maintain skepticism and modesty about your financial expectations if you do start a business. Most people do not enjoy Mark Zuckerberg–level financial success. His is a one-in-a-billion type of story.

However, the long-term financial difference between business ownership and business employment is analogous to the difference between owning a single stock and owning bonds. To know what I mean numerically by that comment, I refer you back to the time series comparing stock and bond returns, put together by Professor Jeremy Siegel, that I referenced in Chapter 14. The financial upside for a successful business owner completely dominates the financial upside potential of most successful employees. There is no upper limit to how much wealth you could build with your own business, whereas an employee will always find his or her compensation capped by a business owner.

Being an employee of someone else's business, of course, can be perfectly rewarding. You can have a nice solid income. But you "are unlikely to" become truly rich.

Exceptions exist to my broad statement. Some "super-managers" rise to the top of companies they did not found, and manage to extract giant paydays. Their stories are one-in-a-million, however, and not the norm. Like I mentioned in Chapter 17 on work, some of my former colleagues on Wall Street are these exceptions, but we're still talking about highly rare one-in-a-thousand type employee compensation.

I'm not sure that "getting really rich" should ever be a personal goal. But I am sure that if that is your goal, you should work on founding your own company as soon as possible, rather than try to get there as an employee of someone else's company.

Tax Advantages

I mentioned in Chapter 10 that the U.S. tax code favors the already wealthy. It also favors entrepreneurs. To give just one example, business owners can choose to pay themselves each year through dividends, potentially at a far lower tax rate than they could as salaried employees. Of course, consult your tax preparer before trying any specific tax-efficient strategy available to entrepreneurs. Saying "I read one time that I could do this tax thing from this guy, in a book . . ." isn't really what you want to have to tell the IRS someday.

In addition, through careful planning, business owners can enjoy tax deductions that salaried employees may not. A vast group of expenses—such as for vehicles, real estate, electronic devices, travel, meals—may be legitimately incurred for a business that you own. Those expenses, in turn, may reduce your annual income, which reduces your tax bill. Again, you'll want to employ a tax preparer or CPA to keep you solidly on the straight and narrow with these tax deductions, but you should know that opportunities exist for the business owner who receives good advice. As always, taxes are not the reason to do something, but you should be aware of their effect on your finances.

Happiness

Finally on the subject of entrepreneurship, I can't prove the following, but I believe it. The most satisfied people in business are the ones who have built their own thing. Entrepreneurs, in my anecdotal experience, are unhappy working for someone else. That unhappiness drives them to found their own company.

The cliché "Do what you love and you will never work a day in your life" overstates the case, but at least approaches what I'm getting at here.

Optimistically speaking, if you can build your own company as an entrepreneur, building your own wealth along the way, you might feel less like you're working and more like you are just being yourself.

Being an entrepreneur will fit some people and not others. It's not a universal rule I insist on. For the second idea relating to wealth, being philanthropic, I feel similarly. This could be an important key to being and feeling wealthy, although I can't claim universality.

Philanthropy

You may be under the mistaken impression that giving time and money to a charitable, or philanthropic purpose, is only for the ultra-wealthy, or the already retired. Be skeptical of that conventional wisdom.

The best way to feel, or to really know you are wealthy, is when you give some of your wealth away. I'm not talking about huge sums of money. Even modest amounts of your time will make you feel rich. Even modest amounts of money can give you that wealthy feeling. In Chapter 19 on estate planning I mention a life hack for setting yourself up to give modest amounts of money, in a professional way. An OK life-cycle model for giving back to a favorite philanthropic cause is to acknowledge you have more time now, and less money. Later, you might end up with more money and less time. That's fine. Give what you can, while you develop more knowledge about the problems, institutions, and solutions in the world.

Do Not Diversify

When it comes to choosing your philanthropic interest, I'd urge the opposite of Chapter 13's advice on investments, specifically regarding diversification. With philanthropy, focusing on the fewest number of causes and institutions will serve you better. Don't diversify your philanthropy.

Be modest about the number of causes you could conceivably support. An infinite number of problems exist in the world. You are just one person with limited time and money. You will likely help more if you humbly decide to focus your efforts, with more profound engagement. You will likely help more if you commit to understanding the problem as best as you can.

Concentration on one problem or one institution gives you the chance to do a deeper dive into barriers and solutions. Why does the problem exist? Why does the problem persist? Why have existing organizations not solved it yet? What are the advantages and disadvantages of existing organizations? How might you apply your talents to help alleviate the problem? How might you support existing organizations with your time, talents, and money? How might you come up with innovative approaches to the problem, inside or outside of existing organizations?

The more you concentrate your energy, talents, and money on the smallest number of problems, the more likely you are to come up with answers to these questions. These questions and answers will help you figure out a way to help the most.

Give to Feel Wealthy

On the issue of philanthropy, I believe the following:

You will always feel poor—no matter the size of your wallet—if you haven't got an hour or a dime to give to something beyond yourself. By extension of that logic, you could have a huge bank account and sizable monetary net worth but still feel broke if you haven't figured out where and how to give some of it back. The rich man with no philanthropic interest will feel a gnawing inside himself. What do I believe in? What do I stand for?

Conversely, you will always feel at least a little bit wealthy if you have got that hour, and that dime, to give. There's no need to wait until the end of your life to enjoy that wealthy feeling. Start now with a little bit of time and a little bit of money. You will feel wealthier.

Finally, when it comes to philanthropy, be optimistic. If you've studied a persistent problem in the world, and you've concentrated your talents and resources on coming up with a way to make it better, you can and will make a difference. Making that difference may be—at the final reckoning—what makes you feel the wealthiest.

What Is Wealthy?

One of the weird truisms of life is that the more money you make or have, the more people you will know in your life who have more than you in the bank, or who earn more than you per year. Comparisons with those moneyed peers will always leave you feeling that you have less than others. The really weird paradoxical truth is that this happens at *every single financial level you might attain*. As a result, it is impossible to be "rich enough" by a pure monetary measure and in comparison with others.

No amount of commas and zeros in a bank account can ensure that you feel, and are, wealthy.

Would I personally still like to wield an American Express Black Card at the posh nightclub like a samurai? Sometimes, maybe. Did I find driving a Maserati around town with my brother one weekend years ago thrilling, and do I wish my net worth allowed for that more often? Kind of, sort of, yes, I'll admit it. When I'm stuck flying economy class, delayed for 2 hours on the runway feeling like sweaty vacuum-packed meat, do I long for a private jet to whisk me away from all this? Of course.

But the Amex, the Maserati, and the jet cannot make me wealthy. In fact, because they cost so much to obtain, they make being wealthy that much more difficult, by my definition.

Wealthy is not an amount of money. It's the amount of time remaining in your life during which you don't have to earn money to provide for your lifestyle needs. It's the freedom to pursue activities that infuse your life with its highest meaning, without regard for what that activity earns. If you have enough in the bank to never have to earn money again, that's step one to being and feeling wealthy. But remain skeptical, because that is not enough.

If you know what activity lights you up and gives everything meaning, that's step two to being and feeling wealthy. Be optimistic that you can discover what that specific activity is, for you. That might be—I hope it is—work. Maybe even a business you started. That might include—again, I hope it does—a philanthropic activity you engage with deeply.

Combine steps one and two, and voila! You are wealthy. Stated as succinctly as I can, what is wealthy?

Wealthy consists of having enough money on a monthly basis to cover your lifestyle costs for the rest of your life, such that you can work at whatever lights you up personally, regardless of the financial compensation for that work.

Getting to this stage of wealthy, for most of us, will take nearly a lifetime. I'm skeptical that most people I know, even the ones with more zeros after their name, have gotten there yet. But this is the goal toward which our financial behavior—heck, our entire life's effort—should aim.

Modestly speaking, I'll admit, I'm not there yet myself. This book was an absolute pleasure to write, however, honestly lighting me up with joy as the highest expression of my life's meaning. I'm optimistic that you, the reader, benefited reading this book as much as I did writing it.

If you did, I have a final favor to ask of you. Please share this book with someone you love who may benefit. Second, please let me know what you liked @Michael_Taylor on Twitter or write to me via the contact page on my website, www.bankers-anonymous.com.

Glossary

Active investing
For mutual funds, active investing means the decision to purchase or exchange securities is made by a manager or team of managers attempting to achieve the best investment results possible within a given investment theme. Because of the need to compensate the manager and support the investment team, actively managed mutual funds tend to have higher management costs than passively invested mutual funds.

After-tax
An adjustment to the value of one's income or investments, taking into account the effect of taxes. To overly simplify, a person earning $40,000 per year owing 10% in taxes could have a $36,000 after-tax income.

After-tax returns
The idea that we should reasonably compare investment results only after taking into consideration the amount of taxes that will need to be paid on that asset once it is sold, or the amount of taxes that will be charged on income from the asset.

Alt-A
An intermediate credit risk designation applied to mortgage borrowers who may be somewhere between subprime and prime, according to FICO scores and other risk factors. Alt-A may also indicate that the borrower has provided limited documentation of his or her income or wealth, resulting in higher interest rates to compensate the lender for the additional risk.

ARM (adjustable-rate mortgage)
A mortgage with a set interest rate for the first 2, 3, or 5 years, but which will readjust annually to a new, possibly higher, interest rate after the fixed period is over. This can be dangerous for borrowers for whom a higher interest rate will make monthly payments unaffordable.

Auto loan

Debt backed by an automobile as collateral. These can be obtained from an auto dealer or from a bank or credit union. Even if you eventually obtain a loan from an auto dealer, it's a good idea to get preapproved for a loan from your bank or credit union before shopping for a car, in order to reduce the number of simultaneous negotiations involved in purchasing a car.

Automation

The absolute number one key to successful savings and investments. We need to "set it and forget it" when it comes to investing in order to overcome our natural human tendency to not save or invest when given a choice. The decision to automate removes the choice and leads to savings and investment success.

Beneficiary

The named recipient of a deceased person's retirement account or life insurance contract.

Bonds

Also commonly known as fixed income. In simplest form, a bond is a loan to a company or government, for a known amount of time and at a contractually obligated interest rate. As an investor, returns come from the repayment of interest and principle over time. Bonds may also be made up of a combination of loans, such as mortgages, creating a bond securitization. If the bond is from a highly rated company or government, the investment is considered not risky.

Budget

Tracking income and expenses, ideally for at least a month at a time, to cover major expenses like housing, transportation costs, and credit card bills.

Capital gains tax

The tax owed by an investor who sells an asset that has appreciated in value since purchase. This applies to assets like stocks, but could also apply to a business or real estate. For example, at a 20% capital gains tax rate, an investor who bought a stock at $5,000 and sold it at $15,000 would owe 20% of the $10,000 gain in the year of the sale, or $2,000.

Car title loans

A typically high-interest loan collateralized by a car. Unlike prime auto loans, these loans are targeted at financially distressed or subprime borrowers and carry high rates of interest.

Cash back financing

A transaction from an auto dealer that allows the purchase to buy a car and also receive cash. This makes no sense financially, as it would only result in a larger loan.

Certificate of deposit (CD)

Typically purchased from a bank or credit union, CDs provide a fixed amount of interest for a set amount of time such as 1 month or 6 months or 2 years. These are a form of fixed income and are very low risk.

Claim
The monetary loss presented to an insurance company for payment in the case of the unexpected insurable event occurring.

Collateralized loan
A loan, such as a car loan or home mortgage or pawn-shop loan, in which the borrower pledges something valuable as a guarantee in case of nonpayment.

Compound interest
The idea that money grows over time and at an increasing pace, as "interest grows on interest."

Consumer Reports
A service providing product comparisons based on cost, reliability, and performance on consumer goods including cars.

Coverage
The maximum payout available in case the unexpected insurable event occurs. The higher the coverage, the more expensive the premium. If you can self-insure through savings and investments, coverages can be kept to a minimum, thus lowering the cost of insurance.

Credit bureaus
Three companies—Equifax, Experian, and TransUnion—that continuously collect data from lenders on experiences with individual borrowers. Their reports are used by lenders for both marketing and risk management purposes. We can and should access our credit reports from these companies when seeking to borrow money, in order to see exactly what banks see when making lending decisions about us.

Credit card
A high-interest, short-term line of credit to which most adults have access. While many "teaser" rates begin at 0% or a low to moderate rate, most credit cards charge much higher rates over time through a combination of stated interest rate, fees, and penalties. In the United States, credit card companies may charge a maximum allowable rate of 29.99%.

Credit union
A business offering traditional banking services such as deposits and loans, but which operates for the benefit of members, rather than as a for-profit entity.

Death
My only 100% personal guarantee in this book!

Deductible
The amount of loss an insured person will endure before the insurance company becomes responsible to pay for the loss. With a $1,000 deductible on a $25,000 claim for homeowner's insurance, for example, the company will pay out $24,000, leaving the first $1,000 loss to the homeowner. If given a choice of deductible, an insured person can choose a higher deductible in order to receive

a lower cost of insurance. This can be a wise choice to save money, as long as the insured has resources to "self-insure," at least to the amount of the deductible.

Discount rate
The mathematical number which, when applied to future amounts of money, translates those payments into an equivalent amount of present-day money. In mathematical terms of the compound interest formula and discounting cash-flows formula, the discount rate serves the same function as yield.

Discounting cashflows
The mathematical technique that underpins banking and insurance, business investment decisions, and is the key tool of all fundamental stock and bond investing.

Diversification
The idea that investors should hold a variety of investments that have different characteristics. The key to having diversification improve your portfolio is that the investment results are not perfectly, or highly, correlated.

Dividends
A share of profits that may be distributed to owners of shares in a for-profit company. Under current income tax law in the United States, dividends are taxed at a lower rate than ordinary income.

Donor-advised fund (DAF)
A low-cost investment vehicle to achieve a tax advantage now for making future charitable gifts, while allowing for time to consider recipients. In addition, through the appointment of trustees such as one's children, the DAF becomes a way to include others in a discussion of one's philanthropic values.

Efficient markets hypothesis
The idea that asset prices adjust extremely quickly to reflect all known information about an investment's prospects. The logical response to the efficient markets hypothesis is to develop deep skepticism about how much "edge" any individual person could have in selecting individual stocks (or other investment products) in attempting to "beat the market." Even if you do not embrace a hardcore version of the efficient markets hypothesis, it is useful to assume it is true in most cases, until proven otherwise.

Emergency fund
The typical advice to new savers to build up a cash buffer for unexpected expenses. Not as useful, in my opinion, as an open line of unused credit, like an unused credit card.

Employer match
The only "free lunch" in the known universe, in which an employer adds money to an employee's retirement account, such as a 401(k) or 403(b) plan.

Entrepreneur
A person who creates an organization that did not exist before to solve a problem.

Entrepreneurship
The act of creating a new line of business that did not exist before. Also, the key to building extraordinary wealth in one's own lifetime.

Envelope trick
The technique for saving money and imposing discipline on spending through placing a fixed amount of cash in an envelope dedicated to specific spending categories like "eating out," "transportation," or "back-to-school clothes."

Equities
The category of investments, like stocks, which represent ownership in for-profit companies, with rights to vote but more importantly, rights to share in future profits, if any. Traditionally the profits of companies are considered volatile and uncertain, so equities represent a high-risk, high-return way to invest.

Estate planning
Legal and tax planning, through documents and discussion, for disposal of your assets, especially after you die. Although taxes are typically a consideration, an even higher consideration should be pursuing an expression of your life's values.

Estate tax
A tax on the value of cash and assets left by a deceased person.

Exchange-traded fund (ETF)
A basket of thematically related investments such as stocks or bonds that may be purchased or sold through a single transaction. Similar to a mutual fund, except that ETFs may be purchased at any time throughout the day at the then-prevailing price. ETFs are typically "passively invested" in the sense that the list of securities will be set ahead of time according to preset criteria, rather than made up according to manager discretion.

Exclusions
The events not covered by insurance, such as suicides within a certain time frame after purchasing for life insurance, or claims for flood damage for most homeowner's insurance.

FICO score
The single score produced by the Fair Isaac Corporation and available for purchase from three consumer credit bureaus that forms a key part of how lenders see borrowers. The score is determined by an algorithm that takes into account historical and current experience borrowing money. It does not take into account factors such as income, employment status, wealth, race, ethnicity, or geography. A 720 or higher score should qualify borrowers for a prime rate loan. Below

a 660 FICO and borrowers may be offered a subprime loan. Between 660 and 720 is sometimes labeled Alt-A and may result in terms between subprime and prime. Borrowers should always know their FICO score before requesting credit.

Financial Infotainment Industrial Complex
The majority of financial media, including print, video, audio, and online. Although it pretends to inform, in aggregate it tends to confuse rather than illuminate. It is a mixture of sales, information, and entertainment and not typically a reliable source of financial guidance.

Fixed annuities
An insurance investment product that provides a fixed monthly or annual income stream, usually for the remaining life of the person, and often guaranteed for a limited amount of time, like 5 or 10 or 20 years. These are a form of fixed income, offer a very low return on investment, and are considered very low risk.

Fixed income
The category of investments, like bonds, annuities, and CDs, which offers a series of contractually obligated cashflows of a known amount for a set amount of time. In traditional form, fixed income is low risk and low return.

Flipping houses
A business activity commonly promoted by the Financial Infotainment Industrial Complex. Usually not a sustainable business idea through an entire economic cycle.

401(k) plan
A tax-advantaged, employer-sponsored retirement account, in which contributions are made directly from an employee's paycheck into an investment account. Contributions may also be matched by employers, making these plans especially attractive. Contribution limits are higher than those of an IRA. The 401(k) plan offerings may be custom-designed to the specification of the for-profit employer's wishes, and as such are relatively expensive to administer and more typically found at larger employers.

403(b) plan
A tax-advantaged, employer-sponsored retirement account available to nonprofit and government employees. Contributions are made directly from an employee's paycheck into an investment account. Contributions may also be matched by employers, making these contributions especially attractive. Contribution limits are higher than those of an IRA.

457 plan
A retirement account available to highly compensated employees of nonprofit organizations. Employees may contribute to, or receive employer contributions to, both a 457 plan and a 403(b) plan simultaneously.

Future value
The monetary worth of money or an asset at some future point in time.

Gold
A shiny collectible metal with decorative value and limited industrial application that nevertheless gets sold by the Financial Infotainment Industrial Complex to the financially naïve as a safe place to protect your wealth. It has no legitimate place in an individual's investment portfolio.

Hawthorne effect (aka observer effect)
The hypothesis that the act of observing a phenomenon will change the behavior of the thing observed. This is the real advantage of budgeting, in my opinion.

HELOC (home equity line of credit)
A revolving credit line, similar to a credit card, that may be drawn down, repaid, and then drawn upon again as needed. This type of line of credit typically is based on a second lien or mortgage upon a home. This can be a powerful advanced-level financial tool for a responsible borrower. Because it is a mortgage on a home, however, a HELOC can be a dangerous tool in the hands of someone who has a history of trouble with debt.

Homeowner's insurance
Insurance commonly required by banks to insure against damage to the property, as well as personal property. Typically excludes protection against floods.

Income tax
The amount of federal, state, and local money owed per year as a result of annual earnings. Understanding the role of income taxes can help us think about the best and most efficient way to earn money.

Inflation
The economic term for the prices of goods and services going up over time. This may be in part because the value of the currency has decreased, or it may just reflect supply and demand of the thing for sale.

Inflation hedge
The idea that a home with a mortgage can act as partial protection in case of unexpectedly high inflation. In that circumstance, the nominal prices of the real estate will increase mostly in line with inflation elsewhere. The mortgage, however, will become worth relatively less, under conditions of high inflation.

Inheritance
Assets received from a deceased person.

Insurance
A financial product properly used to transfer unexpected and catastrophic risks from an individual or business to a company.

Interest rate
The additional money owed by a borrower to a lender, in return for the use of money for a set amount of time. Usually quoted as an annual rate.

Internal rate of return (IRR)
The growth of money in an investment over time. Usually quoted as an annual growth rate. In the mathematical formulas for compound interest and discounting cashflows, yield is an equivalent variable to internal rate of return (IRR), as well as discount rate.

Investment adviser
A professional who, ideally, helps an individual or family formulate a long-term investment plan, and then helps keep to that plan despite what happens in the market. Although frequently paid handsomely for this service, the fees are worth it if they help start an individual on a plan and then stick to that plan. At least 95% of people probably need an investment adviser.

Key man life
A type of life insurance purchased by businesses for important executives, to compensate the company against the risk of the executives' death.

Latte effect
The term popularized by personal finance author David Bach for the idea that each of us spends small amounts of money on a daily or weekly basis on personal luxuries that go practically unnoticed by us. Bach's insight is that these small "latte" purchases add up, in the long run, to huge amounts of forgone savings or investments.

Location, importance of
The number one determinant of price in real estate.

Long-term capital gains
Refers to the amount that would be subject to taxation if the asset were held for a year or more. Under current U.S. tax laws, long-term capital gains are taxed less than short-term capital gains, presumably to reward "investing" rather than "speculating."

Lottery
Legalized gambling organized by the government as a tax on people who are bad at math.

Low-interest debt
Debt offered to prime borrowers, as well as debt lent with collateral, such as a car loan or home mortgage.

Marginal income tax rate
The highest income tax rate to which a person is subject. A person subject to a 30% income tax rate will pay that amount of tax on income earned above a tax bracket threshold. Income earned below the threshold will only be taxed at the

lower rate. Because not all income is taxed at the highest rate, it is considered "marginal," only applying to income above the threshold.

Mortgage
A loan specifically collateralized by real estate. For homes, the typical mortgage can be paid off in 30 years, or somewhat less commonly, 15 years. Mortgages with a schedule different from 15 or 30 years may have a worse interest rate, as the market for these is less common.

Mortgage-interest tax deduction
An income tax deduction, allowing most homeowners to receive a break on annual interest paid for a mortgage. A homeowner who paid $4,000 in mortgage interest over the course of a year and who pays a 25% marginal income tax rate could end up benefiting from this deduction up to 25% of the interest paid, or $1,000.

Mutual fund
A basket of thematically related investments such as stocks or bonds that may be purchased in a single transaction, according to the price of the basket at the end of a trading day. Investors receive over time the blended investment results of the underlying stocks or bonds and pay a management fee to the company that makes the investment selections. The investment theme varies greatly by mutual fund, placing mutual funds along any point on the risk spectrum.

Negative cashflow
In the real estate context, the idea that although it may be considered partially an investment, real estate typically costs money to own, unlike, say, a stock or a bond.

Net worth
A simple measurement of financial wealth, calculated as the sum of all financial and salable assets, minus all debts.

Not risky
Traditionally understood as describing assets that preserve their nominal value under a wide range of scenarios, as well as describing low volatility of results from an investment. Understanding the long-term prospects of a traditional basket of equities and fixed income, however, should help us reevaluate what not risky really means. Traditional "not risky" assets like fixed income typically offer close to zero real return after tax and inflation are taken into consideration.

Passive investing
For mutual funds, passive investing means that the fund will only own a predetermined list of securities according to a set of rules known ahead of time. No human manager intervenes to maximize the investment or try to "beat the market." Because investing is done automatically based on those criteria, management costs of passively invested mutual funds tend to be very low.

Pawn shop loans
A short-term 30-day or 90-day loan backed by the pledge of a valuable personal item. Annual interest rates can exceed 100%. Unlike most similar loans, however, pawn shop loans do not get reported to credit bureaus, as the pawn shop will simply keep the personal item in the event of default on the loan, instead of affecting personal credit of the borrower.

Pay-day loans
Short-term, high-interest loans, secured by a promise to repay when the borrower gets the next paycheck. All-in interest rates can exceed 100% annually.

Philanthropy
Charitable giving, ideally pursued in an undiversified way, and also pursued as an expression of your personal values.

Premium
The monthly or annual amounts paid to the insurance company. This is the cost of insurance.

Present value
The monetary worth of money or an asset in today's terms.

Price per square foot
A common metric for comparing the relative expensiveness or affordability of real estate. It allows for a financial comparison between real estate of different sizes, locations, and styles. As a blunt tool, however, it does not tell us about important considerations such as aesthetics, quality of building, and livability.

Prime
Designation for highest quality lending terms, available typically to borrowers with a FICO score above 720, as well as income, wealth, and employment factors that justify the best terms. Prime loans for homes and automobiles will have relatively low rates of interest.

Real estate tax
A common way local governments raise funds. Varies greatly by state and somewhat by local government.

Real vs. nominal returns
The idea that while the numerical (nominal) price of an asset may be increased by some amount, we need to take into account the effect of inflation on the real return of the asset. For example, an asset that increased in value by a nominal 10% in a year will, in effect, have a negative real return if inflation runs at 11% that year.

Rent vs. buy
A common debate for people who have not owned their own home. My own test is whether you plan to own the house for 5 or more years. Less time than 5 years

and the decision to own, from a financial perspective, becomes relatively more risky. More than 5 years and it will probably work out.

Required minimum distribution (RMD)

The amount that a retired person aged 70.5 or older must withdraw from retirement accounts per year, according to an IRS schedule. The point of the RMD is to make the income received from retirement accounts subject to income taxation in retirement. The RMD is set by determining the expected remaining life of the retiree, according to an actuarial table with the IRS, and dividing the account value by that expected remaining life.

Retirement

The act of leaving one's work. Ideally one does not "live for retirement" but rather works at something from which full retirement isn't even the goal. Because work can confer meaning and attachment to the world, retirement planning should include ways to remain engaged in meaningful work, even after deciding to forgo the need for full compensation for one's work.

Retirement account

Investment accounts that typically offer tax advantages but cannot be withdrawn from (without penalty) until you reach retirement age. Because of the long-time horizon between investing and retiring, these should be concentrated with higher-risk, higher-reward assets to maximize the power of compound interest.

Risky

Traditionally understood as describing the possibility of loss in an investment, as well as the volatility of results from the investment. Understanding the long-term prospects of a traditional basket of equities, however, should help us reevaluate what risky really means. Traditional "risky" assets such as equities, held over the long term, offer such an overwhelming real return advantage over "not risky" assets such as fixed income that the real risk for young people and retirement savers is to not hold equities.

Roth IRA

An individual retirement arrangement available to any individual who earns income in a year. Unlike the traditional IRA, the Roth IRA does not provide income tax relief in the year of contribution. Rather, income withdrawn after retirement may be enjoyed tax free. Investments held inside a Roth IRA are also exempt from taxes such as on dividends and capital gains. Contribution limits on IRAs are relatively low, compared to contribution limits for an employer-sponsored plan such as a 401(k). Upper income earners may be ineligible to make Roth IRA contributions.

SEP-IRA

An employer-sponsored retirement account appropriate for small businesses. The contribution limit per year is relatively high.

Short-term capital gains

Refers to the amount that would be subject to taxation if the asset were held for less than a year. Under current U.S. tax laws, short-term capital gains are taxed at the same rate as ordinary income, which is typically higher than the tax rate on long-term capital gains.

Simple IRA

An employer-sponsored retirement account appropriate for small businesses. These are less flexible than 401(k) plans but are typically simpler and cheaper to administer. Contribution limits are also lower with a simple IRA than for a 401(k) plan.

Stocks

Also commonly known as equities. A stock represents a fractional ownership in a for-profit company, and typically confers rights to vote and share in future profits, if any, in proportion to total ownership in the company. Because the profit of any individual company is uncertain, the investment results of any single stock can be volatile. As an investment, individual stocks are rightly considered risky.

Subprime

Designation for lending terms that may include high interest rates, penalties, and fees. Borrowers with no credit history, limited credit history, or a checkered credit history will tend to only qualify for subprime loans. FICO scores of around 660 or below may result in subprime lending terms.

Subprime car loan

A car loan for borrowers with less than prime credit, usually a FICO score lower than 720. Interest rates may be between 5% or 10% higher, or more, than they are for a prime borrower.

Subprime home loan

A home loan for a borrower with less than prime credit, usually a FICO score lower than 720. Interest rates on subprime home loans could be 5% or more higher than for prime loans.

Tax advance loans

Short-term loans meant to bridge the time between filing taxes for which a refund is due, and the actual receipt of the tax refund. These loans tend to have very high rates of interest.

Taxes

Funds owed to federal, state, and local government. While important, they should never be the primary reason for making a financial decision. Do not let the tail wag the dog.

Taxes, preparing for filing

My rule: Don't do your own taxes if you are no longer a student. You will save money in the long run, and will avoid running afoul of the IRS.

Term life insurance
Insurance purchased to protect against the risk of death for a set amount of time, such as 5, 10 or 20 years, that pays out upon the death of the insured person. Term life insurance isolates the "risk transfer" aspect of life insurance better than whole life, and therefore is typically a better choice.

Time value of money (TVM)
The idea that money in hand today is inherently more valuable than that same amount of money will be in the future. This is partly due to the fact that the future is risky, partly due to the usefulness of money today that can be spent on things today, and partly due to phenomena like inflation, which lessens the value of currency over time.

Traditional IRA
An individual retirement arrangement available to any individual who earns income in a year. The traditional IRA provides a deduction on income tax for qualifying contributors. Investments inside an IRA are also exempt from taxes such as on dividends and capital gains. IRA investors will eventually pay ordinary income taxes on funds withdrawn after retirement. Contribution limits on IRAs are relatively low compared to contribution limits for an employer-sponsored plan such as a 401(k). Income tax deductibility on contributions may phase out for upper income earners.

Transaction costs
The price of buying or selling an investment. Real estate has some of the highest transaction costs of any investment.

Variable annuities
An investment product offered by insurance companies that purports to offer safety through a guaranteed minimum return, but also some high yield if the stock market performs well. Because of the high fees, high commissions for salespeople, and illiquidity of the product, I consider these a garbage product that will mostly enrich the insurance company and their salespeople at your expense.

Warranty
A type of insurance for services or consumer goods to financially compensate the purchaser for losses due to faulty work or damage.

Wealthy
Being wealthy consists of having sufficient assets or cashflow to cover your lifestyle costs on a monthly basis, for the rest of your life, such that you can work at whatever lights you up personally without regard to the level of compensation for that work.

Whole life insurance
Insurance intended to be maintained for life, and to pay out upon the death of the insured, whenever that eventually may occur. Often combined with savings,

lending, and investing concepts such as "accumulated value" and loans to pay premiums, whole life insurance usually violates the pure concept of insurance as a risk transfer. For that reason I prefer term life insurance.

Yield

The investment term that describes the rate of growth of money over time, typically for a specific investment. Usually quoted as an annual growth rate, making it comparable to an interest rate. In mathematical terms, yield is equivalent to internal rate of return (IRR), as well as discount rate.

Zero percent financing

A transaction that allows borrowers to pay no interest on the loan for a period of time. Understanding the time value of money theory, however, we can understand that the only way a zero percent financing transaction makes sense for the seller is if they sell the product at a substantially higher price than they would be willing to sell the product for cash. Commonly offered with large consumer transactions such as furniture and cars.

Selected Bibliography

Books

Bach, David. *The Automatic Millionaire: A Powerful One-Step Plan to Live and Finish Rich.* New York: Broadway Books, 2004.

Clason, George S. *The Richest Man in Babylon.* Reprint Edition by Dauphin Publications, 2015.

Gawande, Atul. *Being Mortal: Medicine and What Matters in the End.* New York: Metropolitan Books, 2014.

Gibran, Kahlil. *The Prophet.* New York: Knopf, 1994.

Graham, Benjamin. *The Intelligent Investor: A Book of Practical Counsel*, rev. ed. New York: Harper, 2006.

Malkiel, Burton G. *A Random Walk Down Wall Street: The Time-Tested Strategy for Successful Investing.* New York: Norton, 2012.

Murray, Nick. *Behavioral Investment Counseling.* New York: Nick Murray Company, 2008.

Murray, Nick. *Simple Wealth, Inevitable Wealth,* 5th ed. New York: Nick Murray Company, 2013.

Schwed, Fred. *Where Are the Customers' Yachts? Or a Good Hard Look at Wall Street.* New York: Wiley, 2006.

Siegel, Jeremy. *Stocks for the Long Run: The Definitive Guide to Financial Market Returns and Long-Term Investment Strategies,* 5th ed. New York: McGraw-Hill Education, 2014.

Tobias, Andrew. *The Only Investment Guide You'll Ever Need.* New York: Mariner Books, 2010.

Online Material and Websites

Brown, Josh. "Should You Be 100% Long Stocks?" Accessed September 1, 2017. http://thereformedbroker.com/2016/02/13/should-you-be-100-long -stocks.

Hultstrom, David. "Ruminations on Being a Financial Professional." Accessed September 1, 2017. http://www.financialarchitectsllc.com/Resources. (The rest of the Financial Architects LLC website has a collection of Hultstrom's own reading, aggregations of others' best research, and homegrown data analysis on investment management. There are multiple college course's worth of original material and thoughtful analysis here.)

Jeremy Siegel website: http://www.jeremysiegel.com/index.cfm/fuseaction /Resources.ListResources/type/chart.cfm. (Data on stock, bond, and gold returns.)

Index

About the Author

Michael C. Taylor sold bonds on Wall Street, founded and closed a private investment business, and dedicates himself to the mission of teaching, consulting, and writing about finance. Michael writes a weekly column for the *San Antonio Express News* and *Houston Chronicle* and founded the finance blog www.bankers-anonymous.com. A graduate of Harvard College, he lives with his family in San Antonio, Texas.